CIMA™

How to access your on-line resources

Kaplan Financial students will have a MyKaplan account and these extra resources will be available to you online. You do not need to register again, as this process was completed when you enrolled. If you are having problems accessing online materials, please ask your course administrator.

If you are not studying with Kaplan and did not purchase your book via a Kaplan website, to unlock your extra online resources please go to www.en-gage.co.uk (even if you have set up an account and registered books previously). You will then need to enter the ISBN number (on the title page and back cover) and the unique pass key number contained in the scratch panel below to gain access.

You will also be required to enter additional information during this process to set up or confirm your account details.

If you purchased via the Kaplan Publishing website you will automatically receive an e-mail invitation to register your details and gain access to your content. If you do not receive the e-mail or book content, please contact Kaplan Publishing.

Your code and information

This code can only be used once for the registration of one book online. This registration and your online content will expire when the final sittings for the examinations covered by this book have taken place. Please allow one hour from the time you submit your book details for us to process your request.

Please scratch the film to access your unique code.

hply-63r8-l386-OAmb

Please be aware that this code is case-sensitive and you will need to include the dashes within the passcode, but not when entering the ISBN.

KAPLAN PUBLISHING

CIMA 2019 Professional Examinations

Operational Level

Subject P1

Management Accounting

EXAM PRACTICE KIT

CIMA PUBLISHING

KAPLAN PUBLISHING

British Library Cataloguing-in-Publication Data

A catalogue record for this book is available from the British Library.

Published by:

Kaplan Publishing UK
Unit 2 The Business Centre
Molly Millar's Lane
Wokingham
Berkshire
RG41 2QZ

ISBN: 978-1-78740-208-9

CONTENTS

Quality and accuracy are of the utmost importance to us so if you spot an error in any of our products, please send an email to mykaplanreporting@kaplan.com with full details.

Our Quality Co-ordinator will work with our technical team to verify the error and take action to ensure it is corrected in future editions.

INDEX TO QUESTIONS AND ANSWERS

OBJECTIVE TEST QUESTIONS

EXAM TECHNIQUES

COMPUTER-BASED ASSESSMENT

Golden rules

1. Make sure you have completed the compulsory 15-minute tutorial before you start the test. This tutorial is available through the CIMA website and focusses on the functionality of the exam. You cannot speak to the invigilator once you have started.
2. These exam practice kits give you plenty of exam style questions to practise so make sure you use them to fully prepare.
3. Attempt all questions, there is no negative marking.
4. Double check your answer before you put in the final answer although you can change your response as many times as you like.
5. Not all questions will be multiple choice questions (MCQs) – you may have to fill in missing words or figures.
6. Identify the easy questions first and get some points on the board to build up your confidence.
7. Attempt 'wordy' questions first as these may be quicker than the computation style questions. This will relieve some of the time pressure you will be under during the exam.
8. If you don't know the answer, flag the question and attempt it later. In your final review before the end of the exam try a process of elimination.
9. Work out your answer on the whiteboard provided first if it is easier for you. There is also an onscreen 'scratch pad' on which you can make notes. You are not allowed to take pens, pencils, rulers, pencil cases, phones, paper or notes into the testing room.

SYLLABUS GUIDANCE, LEARNING OBJECTIVES AND VERBS

A CIMA 2019 PROFESSIONAL QUALIFICATION

Details regarding the content of the CIMA 2019 professional qualification can be located within the CIMA 2019 professional qualification syllabus document.

You can use the following diagram showing the whole structure of your qualification to help you keep track of your progress. Make sure you carefully review the 2019 CIMA syllabus transition rules and seek appropriate advice if you are unsure about your progression through the qualification.

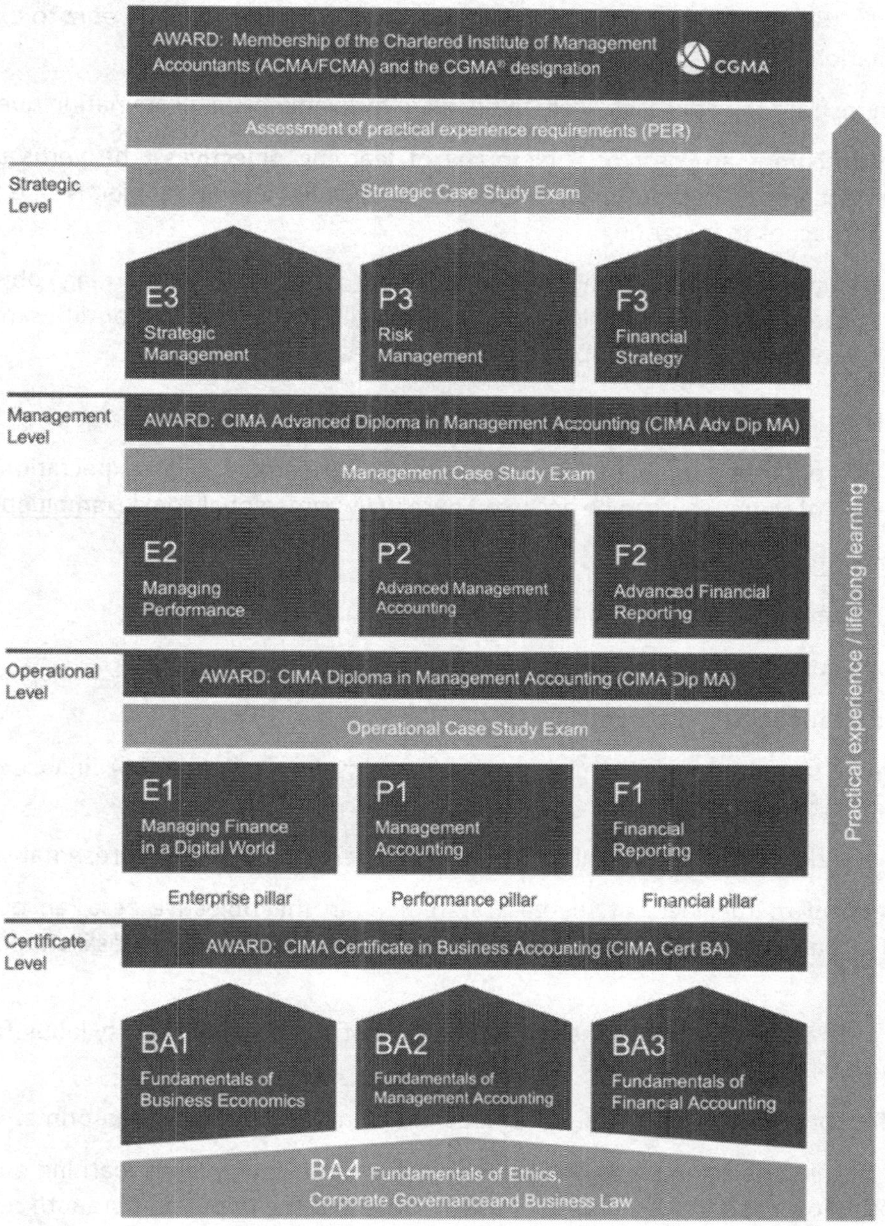

Reproduced with permission from CIMA

B STUDY WEIGHTINGS

A percentage weighting is shown against each exam content area in the exam blueprint. This is intended as a guide to the proportion of study time each topic requires.

All component learning outcomes will be tested.

The weightings do not specify the number of marks that will be allocated to topics in the examination.

C LEARNING OUTCOMES

Each subject within the qualification is divided into a number of broad syllabus topics. The topics contain one or more lead learning outcomes, related component learning outcomes and indicative knowledge content.

A learning outcome has two main purposes:

1 to define the skill or ability that a well-prepared candidate should be able to exhibit in the examination

2 to demonstrate the approach likely to be taken by examiners in examination questions.

The learning outcomes are part of a hierarchy of learning objectives. The verbs used at the beginning of each learning outcome relate to a specific learning objective, e.g. Evaluate alternative approaches to budgeting.

The verb 'evaluate' indicates a high-level learning objective. As learning objectives are hierarchical, it is expected that at this level students will have knowledge of different budgeting systems and methodologies and be able to apply them.

The examination blueprints and representative task statements

CIMA have also published examination blueprints giving learners clear expectations regarding what is expected of them. This can be accessed here www.cimaglobal.com/examblueprints

The blueprint is structured as follows:

- Exam content sections (reflecting the syllabus document)
- Lead and component outcomes (reflecting the syllabus document)
- Representative task statements.

A representative task statement is a plain English description of what a CIMA finance professional should know and be able to do.

The content and skill level determine the language and verbs used in the representative task.

CIMA will test up to the level of the task statement in the objective test (an objective test question on a particular topic could be set at a lower level than the task statement in the blueprint).

The format of the objective test blueprints follows that of the published syllabus for the 2019 CIMA Professional Qualification.

Weightings for content sections are also included in the individual subject blueprints.

A list of the learning objectives and the verbs that appear in the syllabus learning outcomes and examinations follows and these will help you to understand the depth and breadth required for a topic and the skill level the topic relates to.

APPROACH TO REVISION

Stage 1: Assess areas of strengths and weaknesses

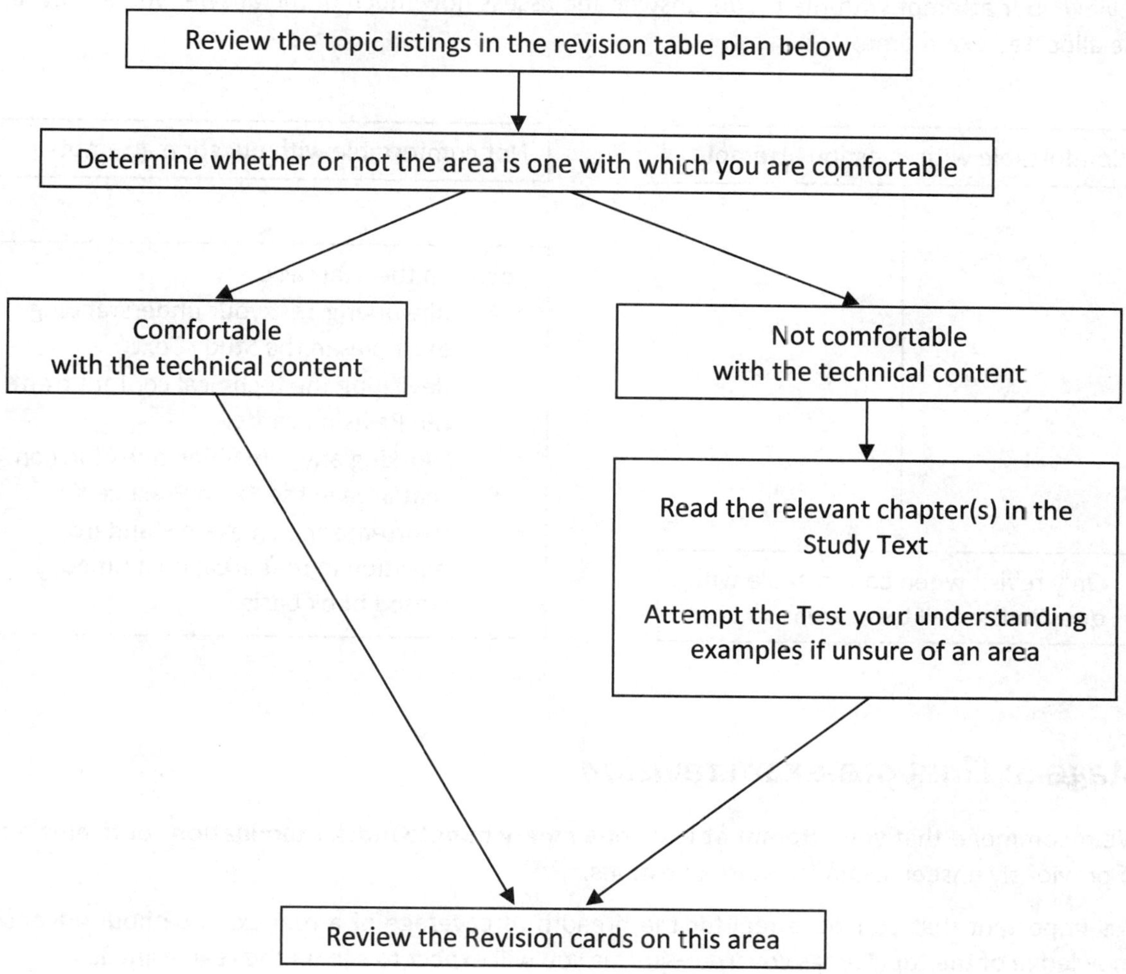

Stage 2: Question practice

Follow the order of revision of topics as recommended in the revision table plan below and attempt the questions in the order suggested.

Try to avoid referring to text books and notes and the model answer until you have completed your attempt.

Try to answer the question in the allotted time.

Review your attempt with the model answer and assess how much of the answer you achieved in the allocated exam time.

Comfortable with question attempt

→ Only revisit when comfortable with questions on all topic areas

Not comfortable with question attempts

→ Focus on these areas by:

- Reworking Test your understanding examples in the Study Text
- Revisiting the technical content from the Revision cards
- Working any remaining questions on that area in the Exam Practice Kit
- Reattempting an exam standard question in that area, on a timed, closed book basis

Stage 3: Final pre-exam revision

We recommend that you **attempt at least one ninety minute mock examination** containing a set of previously unseen exam standard questions.

It is important that you get a feel for the breadth of coverage of a real exam without advanced knowledge of the topic areas covered – just as you will expect to see on the real exam day.

Ideally a mock examination offered by your tuition provider should be sat in timed, closed book, real exam conditions.

SYLLABUS GRIDS

P1: Management Accounting

What the finance function does

Content weighting

Content area		Weighting
A	Cost accounting for decision and control	30%
B	Budgeting and budgetary control	25%
C	Short-term commercial decision-making	30%
D	Risk and uncertainty in the short term	15%
		100%

P1A: Cost accounting for decision and control

This section is about understanding why costing is done and what it is used for. It introduces candidates to the basic building blocks of costing and how to apply them in the costing methods and techniques organisations use. In a fast-changing digital world this understanding is critical and can enable candidates to develop their own ways of calculating costs when existing methods are no longer appropriate. Digital costing is introduced in this section.

Lead outcome	Component outcome	Topics to be covered	Explanatory notes
1. Distinguish between the different rationales for costing.	a. Define costing b. Distinguish between the rationales for costing	• Inventory valuation • Profit reporting • Cost management and transformation • Decision-making	This seeks to address the following pertinent questions: What are reasons for calculating costs? What types of costs are appropriate for a particular purpose and why?
2. Apply the main costing concepts to organisations and cost objects.	a. Explain the main costing concepts b. Apply costing concepts to different organisations and cost objects	• Cost elements • Costs structure • Cost behaviour • Cost drivers • Costing applied to different types of organisations • Costing applied to digital cost objects	Examine the basic building blocks of costing and how they apply to different types of organisations and operating contexts (e.g., manufacturing and service sectors). How has the digital world affected the nature of these building blocks of costing?
3. Apply costing methods to determine the costs for different purposes.	Apply the following: a. Cost accumulation, allocation, apportionment and absorption b. Standard costing c. Variance analysis (without mix and yield variance) d. Activity based costing e. Digital costing	• Trace, classify and allocate costs • Marginal costing • Absorption costing • Price and rate variances • Usage and efficiency variances • Interpretation of variances • Product and service costing using ABC • Advantages of ABC over other costing systems • Features of digital costing	Investigate how costs are traced, classified, accumulated, allocated, apportioned and absorbed to arrive at the costs of a product, service or other cost object. Calculate the costs of products or services using various costing methods. Determine which costing methods are appropriate and why?

P1B: Budgeting and budgetary control

Taken together, budgeting and budgetary control is one way the finance function enables and shapes how organisations create and preserve value. This section examines the various reasons organisations prepare and use budgets, how the budgets are prepared, the types and sources of data, the technologies used to improve the quality of budgets, how budgets are implemented and the impact on the people who work with the organisation.

Lead outcome	Component outcome	Topics to be covered	Explanatory notes
1. Distinguish between the different rationales for budgeting.	a. Explain the role of budgets. b. Distinguish between the different rationales for budgeting.	• Planning • Communication • Coordination • Motivation • Control	Why do organisations prepare budgets? In what ways are the different rationales for preparing budgets compatible with each other? How do organisations get the most out the budgeting process?
2. Prepare budgets.	a. Explain forecasting and its relationship with budgeting. b. Prepare master budgets. c. Conduct what-if analysis in budgeting. d. Describe the technologies available for improving budgeting.	• Time series and trend analysis to forecast sales volumes • Components of master budgets and their interaction with each other • Limiting factors • Stress testing budgets • Big data analytics and budgets • Alternative approaches to budgeting	What is the process by which budgets are prepared? What types of budgets are required by organisations? What data do they use and where do they get the data from? How are those budgets prepared and presented? What technologies are available for improving the quality of the budgets?
3. Discuss budgetary control.	Discuss: a. The concept of budgetary control b. Human dimensions of budgeting	• Feedback and feedforward control • Flexed budgets • Target setting and motivation • Controllable and uncontrollable outcomes • Dysfunctional behaviours in budgeting • Ethical considerations in budgeting	What is budgetary control? Describe and discuss how and why the budgetary control system provides feedback and feedforward to the organisation. What are the behavioural impacts of budgetary control and how are they managed?

P1C: Short-term commercial decision-making

Organisations cannot foresee every opportunity that might arise during their operations, so they need mechanisms by which to identify and take advantage of these opportunities as they arise. The primary objective of this section is to guide candidates in how to do this in the short term through effective decision-making. The finance function supports such decisions (e.g., pricing and product choice) using techniques such as relevant revenue and cost analysis and break- even analysis. Candidates are introduced to these techniques and the concepts that underpin the techniques. They are expected to be able to apply the techniques to support short-term decision-making.

Lead outcome	Component outcome	Topics to be covered	Explanatory notes
1. Describe the main types of short-term decisions made by organisations.	a. Describe pricing and revenue maximising decisions. b. Describe product decisions.	• Marginal and full cost recovery for pricing decisions • Differences in pricing and revenue maximisation for the short term and long term • Product mix	Describe the types of short-term decisions organisations make and the circumstances that give rise to them. What do these short-term decisions seek to achieve? How important are they to performance of organisations? The emphasis is on both revenue and costs.
2. Explain the underlying concepts used for short-term decision-making.	a. Explain the objectives of decision-making. b. Explain the underlying concepts of short-term decision-making.	• Implications of commercial decision-making in the short term • Relevant revenues • Relevant costs • Difference with profit reporting	What are the objectives and underlying concepts that are used to guide short-term decision-making and why? Distinguish between those concepts of revenue, costs and information from other concepts.
3. Apply appropriate techniques to support short-term decisions.	Apply the following to support short-term decision-making: a. Relevant cost analysis b. Break-even analysis c. Product mix decisions with constraints d. Data and technology	• Make or buy decisions • Discontinuation decisions • Multi-product break-even analysis • Use of data and technology to analyse product mix decisions • Ethical considerations in short-term decision-making	Use data (financial and non-financial) and the appropriate concepts and techniques to support decision-making to achieve organisational objectives of value creation and preservation.

P1D: Risk and uncertainty in the short term

Budgets and decisions focus on the future. This introduces uncertainties and risks that need to be identified, assessed and managed. The aim of this section is to help candidates identify, assess and manage the risks and uncertainties associated with the short term.

Lead outcome	Component outcome	Topics to be covered	Explanatory notes
1. Apply basic risk management tools in the short term.	a. Explain nature of risk and uncertainty in short term. b. Apply basic sensitivity analysis to budgeting and short-term decision-making.	• Stress testing • Sensitivity and what-if analysis • Probability distributions • Decision trees	What types of risks and uncertainties do organisations face when preparing and implementing budgets and when making short-term decisions? How are those risks and uncertainties identified, assessed and managed?

Information concerning formulae and tables will be provided via the CIMA website: www.cimaglobal.com.

Section 1

OBJECTIVE TEST QUESTIONS

COST ACCOUNTING FOR DECISION AND CONTROL

RATIONALE FOR COSTING

1 **Which of the following is NOT one of the main purposes of management accounting?**

A Planning

B Reporting

C Decision Making

D Controlling

2 **Do the comments below relate to management or financial accounting? (*tick the correct system)***

	Management accounting	Financial accounting
Uses only historical data		
Is carried out at the discretion of management		
Uses non-financial information		
Aids planning within the organisation		

3 **Which TWO of the following would normally be carried out by strategic level management?**

	Strategic?
Making day-to-day decisions about the running of a department	
Defining the objectives of the company	
Deciding in which markets to operate	
Deciding about how to compete within their chosen markets	
Inventory control	

4 **Direct costs are:**

A costs which can be identified with a cost centre but not identified to a single cost unit

B costs which can be economically identified with a single cost unit

C costs which can be identified with a single cost unit, but it is not economic to do so

D costs incurred as a direct result of a particular decision

5 Which of the following descriptions best suits the graph below?

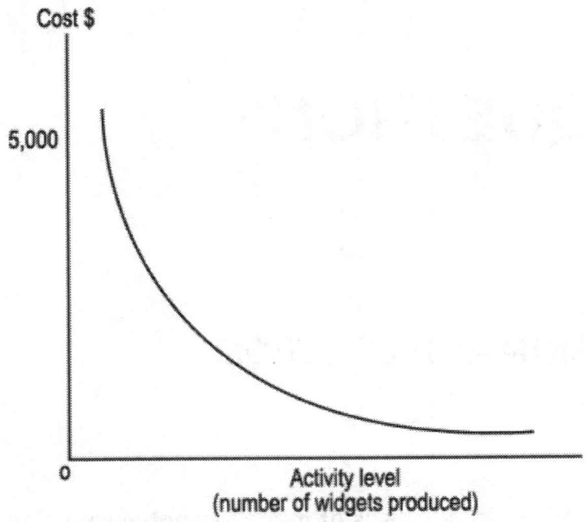

A Total fixed costs

B Total variable costs

C Variable cost per unit

D Fixed cost per unit

6 Which of the following would be classified as direct labour?

A An HR manager in a company servicing cars

B Builder in a construction company

C General manager in a DIY shop

D Maintenance manager in a company producing cameras

TRADITIONAL COSTING

7 A business reported a marginal costing profit of $45,000 last period. Its inventory values for the period were as follows:

	$
Opening inventory	16,000
Closing inventory	20,800

If the business had used absorption costing, the inventory values would have been as follows:

	$
Opening inventory	28,000
Closing inventory	36,400

What would have been the reported profit using absorption costing?

A $41,400

B $48,600

C $57,000

D $60,600

8 A company has a budget to produce 5,000 units of Product B in December. The budget for December shows that, for Product B, the opening inventory will be 400 units and the closing inventory will be 900 units. The monthly budgeted production cost data for Product B for December is as follows:

Variable direct costs per unit	$6.00
Variable production overhead costs per unit	$3.50
Total fixed production overhead costs	$29,500

The company absorbs overheads on the basis of the budgeted number of units produced.

The budgeted profit for Product B for December, using ABSORPTION COSTING, is:

A $2,950 lower than it would be using marginal costing

B $2,950 greater than it would be using marginal costing

C $4,700 lower than it would be using marginal costing

D $4,700 greater than it would be using marginal costing

9 A company operates a standard absorption costing system. The budgeted fixed production overheads for the company for the latest year were $330,000 and budgeted output was 220,000 units. At the end of the company's financial year the total of the fixed production overheads debited to the Fixed Production Overhead Control Account was $260,000 and the actual output achieved was 200,000 units.

The under/over absorption of overheads was:

A $40,000 over absorbed

B $40,000 under absorbed

C $70,000 over absorbed

D $70,000 under absorbed

10 A business manufactures a single product which sells for $45 per unit. The budgeted data for the latest period are as follows:

Production and sales volume	2,000 units
	$
Material cost	13,500
Direct labour cost	11,800
Production overhead	32,400
Non-production overhead	21,900

Actual production volume and costs were as budgeted for the period but the actual sales volume achieved was 1,800 units. There was no inventory at the beginning of the period.

The profit for the period using absorption costing is $_____

11 Which of the following statements are correct (*tick all that apply*)?

		Correct?
(i)	A cost driver is any factor that causes a change in the cost of an activity.	
(ii)	For long-term variable overhead costs, the cost driver will be the volume of activity.	
(iii)	Traditional absorption costing tends to under-allocate overhead costs to low-volume products.	

12 A business manufactures a single product which sells for $45 per unit. The budgeted data for the latest period are as follows:

Production and sales volume	2,000 units
	$
Material cost	13,500
Direct labour cost	11,800
Production overhead	32,400
Non-production overhead	21,900

Actual production volume and costs were as budgeted for the period but the actual sales volume achieved was 1,800 units. There was no inventory at the beginning of the period.

The profit for the period using marginal costing is $_____

13 T uses a standard labour hour rate to charge its overheads to its clients' work. During the last annual reporting period production overheads were under-absorbed by $19,250. The anticipated standard labour hours for the period were 38,000 hours while the standard hours actually charged to clients were 38,500. The actual production overheads incurred in the period were $481,250.

The budgeted production overheads for the period were:

A $456,000

B $462,000

C $475,000

D $498,000

14 WTD Ltd produces a single product. The management currently uses marginal costing but is considering using absorption costing in the future.

The budgeted fixed production overheads for the period are $500,000. The budgeted output for the period is 2,000 units. There were 800 units of opening inventory at the beginning of the period and 500 units of closing inventory at the end of the period.

If absorption costing principles were applied, the profit for the period compared to the marginal costing profit would be:

A $75,000 higher

B $75,000 lower

C $125,000 higher

D $125,000 lower

15 **Overheads will always be over-absorbed when:**

A actual output is higher than budgeted output

B actual overheads incurred are higher than the amount absorbed

C actual overheads incurred are lower than the amount absorbed

D budgeted overheads are lower than the overheads absorbed

16 X Ltd has two production departments, Assembly and Finishing, and two service departments, Stores and Maintenance.

Stores provides the following service to the production departments: 60% to Assembly and 40% to Finishing.

Maintenance provides the following service to the production and service departments: 40% to Assembly, 45% to Finishing and 15% to Stores.

The budgeted information for the year is as follows:

Budgeted fixed production overheads	
Assembly	$100,000
Finishing	$150,000
Stores	$50,000
Maintenance	$40,000
Budgeted output	100,000 units

At the end of the year after apportioning the service department overheads, the total fixed production overheads debited to the Assembly department's fixed production overhead control account were $180,000.

The actual output achieved was 120,000 units.

The under-/over-absorption of fixed production overheads for the Assembly department is $_______

17 Summary results for Y Limited for March are shown below:

	$000	*Units*
Sales revenue	820	
Variable production costs	300	
Variable selling costs	105	
Fixed production costs	180	
Fixed selling costs	110	
Production in March		1,000
Opening inventory		0
Closing inventory		150

Using *marginal costing*, the profit for March was:

A $170,000

B $185,750

C $197,000

D $229,250

18 GH produces three models of speedboat for sale to the retail market. GH currently operates a standard absorption costing system. Budgeting information for next year is given below:

Model of speedboat	*Superior*	*Deluxe*	*Ultra*	*Total*
	$000	$000	$000	$000
Sales	54,000	86,400	102,000	242,400
Direct material	17,600	27,400	40,200	85,200
Direct labour	10,700	13,400	16,600	40,700
Production overhead				69,600
Gross profit				46,900

	Superior	*Deluxe*	*Ultra*
Production/sales (number of boats)	1,000	1,200	800
Machine hours per boat	100	200	300

The production overhead cost is absorbed using a machine hour rate.

The total gross profit for the Deluxe speedboat using absorption costing is $_______

ACTIVITY BASED COSTING

19 **A food-processing company operates an activity based costing (ABC) system. Determine whether the following would be classified as a facility- or product-sustaining activity *(place a tick in the box corresponding to any that would apply)*?**

	Facility-sustaining	*Product-sustaining*
(i) General staff administration		
(ii) Plant management		
(iii) Technical support for individual products and services		
(iv) Updating of product specification database		
(v) Property management		

20 P operates an activity based costing (ABC) system to attribute its overhead costs to cost objects.

In its budget for the year ending 31 August 20X6, the company expected to place a total of 2,895 purchase orders at a total cost of $110,010. This activity and its related costs were budgeted to occur at a constant rate throughout the budget year, which is divided into 13 four-week periods.

During the four-week period ended 30 June 20X6, a total of 210 purchase orders were placed at a cost of $7,650.

The over-recovery of these costs for the four-week period was:

A $330

B $350

C $370

D $390

21 DRP has recently introduced an Activity Based Costing system. It manufactures three products:

	Product D	*Product R*	*Product P*
Budgeted annual production (units)	100,000	100,000	50,000
Batch size (units)	100	50	25
Machine set-ups per batch	3	4	6
Purchase orders per batch	2	1	1
Processing time per unit (minutes)	2	3	3
Budgeted number of batches	1,000	2,000	2,000

Three cost pools have been identified. Their budgeted costs for 20X4 are as follows:

Machine set-up costs $150,000

Purchasing of materials $70,000

Processing $80,000

The cost per unit attributed to Product R for machine set ups is $_____

22 KY makes three products and uses an activity based costing system. The stores receiving costs, which are driven by the number of component deliveries, make up $6,840 of the total production overhead cost.

Driver analysis for KY revealed the following information:

Product	*X*	*Y*	*Z*
Budgeted production (units)	1,000	1,200	800
Number of component deliveries	500	600	800
Number of issues from stores	4,000	5,000	7,000

The total cost attributed to Product Y for component deliveries using the proposed activity based costing system is $_______

23 LMN has recently introduced an Activity Based Costing system. It manufactures three products:

	Product L	*Product M*	*Product N*
Budgeted annual production (units)	300,000	300,000	150,000
Batch size (units)	300	150	75
Machine set-ups per batch	4	2	5
Purchase orders per batch	2	3	2
Processing time per unit (minutes)	4	6	6
Budgeted number of batches	5,000	4,000	4,000

Three cost pools have been identified. Their budgeted costs for the year are as follows:

Machine set-up costs $250,000

Purchasing of materials $105,000

Processing $156,000

The cost per unit attributed to Product L for processing time is $_____

24 HZ makes three products and is considering changing to an activity based costing system. The quality inspection costs make up $14,140 of the total production overhead cost.

Driver analysis for HZ revealed the following information:

Product	*A*	*B*	*C*
Budgeted production	1,000	1,200	800
Production units per production run	5	4	2
Quality inspections per production run	10	20	30

The total cost attributed to Product C for quality inspections using an activity based costing system is $_______

25 **Which of the following explains why an activity based costing system may produce more accurate product costs than a traditional absorption costing system?**

Cost	*Advantage?*
Better cost control is possible	
Arbitrary allocations of costs are avoided	
Better product pricing is possible	
The choice of cost drivers is easy	
Can be applied to service companies	

OTHER ELEMENTS OF COSTING

26 Company B uses a throughput accounting system. The details of product X per unit are as follows:

Selling price	€50
Material cost	€16
Conversion costs	€20
Time on bottleneck resource	8 minutes

The return per hour for product X is:

A €105

B €225

C €255

D €375

27 A company can produce many types of product but is currently restricted by the number of labour hours available on a particular machine. At present this limitation is set at 12,000 hours per annum. One type of product requires materials costing $5 which are then converted to a final product that sells for $12. Each unit of this product takes 45 minutes to produce on the machine. The conversion costs for the factory are estimated to be $144,000 per annum.

The throughput accounting ratio for this product is _____ *(answer to three decimal places)*.

28 A company produces two products, S and T, which pass through two production processes, X and Y. The time taken to make each product in each process is:

	Product S	*Product T*
Process X	5 mins	7.5 mins
Process Y	18 mins	12 mins

The company operates a 15-hour day and have an average downtime each day of:

Process X	1.5 hours
Process Y	1.0 hours

The costs and revenue for each unit of each product are:

	Product S	*Product T*
	$	$
Direct materials	20.00	20.00
Direct labour	18.00	14.00
e overhead	4.00	4.00
Fixed costs	5.00	4.00
Total cost	47.00	42.00
Selling price	$95.00	$85.00

Sales demand restricts the output of S and T to 50 and 80 units a day respectively.

Process ___ *(enter X or Y)* is the bottleneck process.

29 **What is defined as 'an activity within an organisation which has a lower capacity than preceding or subsequent activities, thereby limiting throughput'?**

A Bottleneck

B Constraint

C Limiting factor

D Restraint

30 The following data relate to a manufacturing company. At the beginning of August there was no inventory. During August 2,000 units of Product X were produced, but only 1,750 units were sold. The financial data for Product X for August were as follows:

	$
Materials	40,000
Labour	12,600
Variable production overheads	9,400
Fixed production overheads	22,500
Variable selling costs	6,000
Fixed selling costs	19,300
Total costs for X for August	109,800

The value of inventory of X at 31 August using a throughput accounting approach is $_______

31 A manufacturing company recorded the following costs in October for Product X:

	$
Direct materials	20,000
Direct labour	6,300
Variable production overhead	4,700
Fixed production overhead	19,750
Variable selling costs	4,500
Fixed distribution costs	16,800
Total costs incurred for Product X	72,050

During October 4,000 units of Product X were produced but only 3,600 units were sold. At the beginning of October there was no inventory.

The value of the inventory of Product X at the end of October using throughput accounting was:

A $630

B $1,080

C $1,100

D $2,000

32 A business manufactures a single product which sells for $45 per unit. The budgeted data for the latest period are as follows:

Production and sales volume	2,000 units
	$
Material cost	13,500
Direct labour cost	11,800
Production overhead	32,400
Non-production overhead	21,900

Actual production volume and costs were as budgeted for the period but the actual sales volume achieved was 1,800 units. There was no inventory at the beginning of the period.

The profit for the period using throughput accounting is $_____

33 S Ltd manufactures three products, A, B and C. The products use a series of different machines but there is a common machine, P, that is a bottleneck.

The selling price and standard cost for each product for the forthcoming year is as follows:

	A	*B*	*C*
	$	$	$
Selling price	200	150	150
Direct materials	41	20	30
Conversion costs	55	40	66
Machine P – minutes	12	10	7

The return per hour for Product B is $______

34 Which of the following statements regarding digital products is NOT true?

A The high marginal cost of digital products makes them difficult to price

B The life span of digital products can vary greatly

C There are often recurring costs for digital products

D Determining cost drivers for digital products can be very difficult

35 A company with audio expertise has had great success in selling physical testing equipment to amateurs who want to personalise their home listening experience. It is now considering providing the testing software through a downloadable mobile application.

Consider whether the following are likely to be higher or lower for the mobile phone application than for the existing physical equipment:

	Higher	**Lower**
The life span of the product		
The total labour costs		
Inventory costs		
Infrastructure costs		

36 Which of the following is unlikely to be used when costing digital products?

A Marginal costing

B Absorption costing

C Activity based costing

D Target costing

37 Which of the following is not a typical feature of digital costing?

A Prices are obtained electronically from markets

B Systems are integrated with customer systems

C Intelligence capabilities are built in

D The product cost may constantly change

38 Consider whether the following statements about digital costing are true or false:

	True	**False**
There is a focus on a smaller number of suppliers		
Fewer overhead drivers are used		
Large volumes of data are processed		
The digital cost can be created very quickly		

VARIANCE ANALYSIS

39 A manufacturer expects to use 4 kg of material (at a cost of $5 per kg) on each of its produced units.

Budgeted production was for 5,000 units of a single product. In January, the manufacturer actually spent $82,764 making 4,400 units of its product and used 16,720 kg of material.

To the nearest $, the favourable materials price variance for April is $_______

40 Which of the following best describes a basic standard?

A A standard set at an ideal level, which makes no allowance for normal losses, waste and machine downtime

B A standard which assumes an efficient level of operation, but which includes allowances for factors such as normal loss, waste and machine downtime

C A standard which is kept unchanged over a period of time

D A standard which is based on current price levels

The following data relate to Questions 41 and 42.

X40 is one of many items produced by the manufacturing division. Its standard cost is based on estimated production of 10,000 units per month. The standard cost schedule for one unit of X40 shows that 2 hours of direct labour are required at $15 per labour hour. The variable overhead rate is $6 per direct labour hour. During April, 11,000 units were produced; 24,000 direct labour hours were worked and charged; $336,000 was spent on direct labour; and $180,000 was spent on variable overheads.

---

41 The direct labour rate variance for April is:

A $20,000 Favourable

B $22,000 Favourable

C $24,000 Adverse

D $24,000 Favourable

42 The variable overhead efficiency variance for April is:

A $12,000 Adverse

B $12,000 Favourable

C $15,000 Adverse

D $15,000 Favourable

The following data relate to Questions 43 and 44.

X Ltd operates a standard costing system and absorbs fixed overheads on the basis of machine hours. Details of budgeted and actual figures are as follows:

	Budget	*Actual*
Fixed overheads	$2,500,000	$2,010,000
Output	500,000 units	440,000 units
Machine hours	1,000,000 hours	900,000 hours

43 The fixed overhead expenditure variance is

A $190,000 favourable

B $250,000 adverse

C $300,000 adverse

D $490,000 favourable

44 The fixed overhead volume variance is

A $190,000 favourable

B $250,000 adverse

C $300,000 adverse

D $490,000 favourable)

45 Y has set the current budget for operating costs for its delivery vehicles, using the formula described below. Analysis has shown that the relationship between miles driven and total monthly vehicle operating costs is described in the following formula:

$$y = \$800 + \$0.0002x^2$$

where

y is the total monthly operating cost of the vehicles, and

x is the number of miles driven each month

The budget for vehicle operating costs needs to be adjusted for expected inflation in vehicle operating costs of 3%, which is not included in the relationship shown above.

The delivery mileage for September was 4,100 miles, and the total actual vehicle operating costs for September were $5,000.

The total vehicle operating cost variance for September was closest to:

A $713 Adverse

B $737 Adverse

C $777 Adverse

D $838 Adverse

46 L uses a standard costing system. The standard cost card for one of its products shows that the product should use 6 kgs of material P per finished unit, and that the standard price per kg is $6.75. L values its inventory of materials at standard prices.

During November 20X1, when the budgeted production level was 2,000 units, 2,192 units were made. The actual quantity of material P used was 13,050 kgs and material L inventories were reduced by 500 kgs. The cost of the material L which was purchased was $72,900.

The material price and usage variances for November 20X1 were:

	Price	*Usage*
A	15,185.50 (F)	450.00 (F)
B	11,812.50 (F)	688.50 (F)
C	15,187.50 (F)	450.00 (A)
D	11,812.50 (F)	688.50 (A)

47 A manufacturer spent $244,000 on 9,760 hours of labour producing 6,000 units. However, only 9,480 hours were actually worked by labour. Labour should have taken 1.6 hours per unit at a standard rate of $24 per hour.

What is the value of the adverse labour idle time variance?

A $2,880

B $3,000

C $6,720

D $7,000

48 R uses a standard costing system and has the following labour cost standard in relation to one of its products:

10 hours skilled labour at $9.50 per hour = $95.00

During March 20X9, 6,200 of these products were made which was 250 units less than budgeted. The labour cost incurred was $596,412 and the number of direct labour hours worked was 62,890. The direct labour variances for the month were:

	Rate	*Efficiency*
A	$1,043 (F)	$8,900 (A)
B	$7,412 (F)	$8,455 (A)
C	$1,043 (F)	$8,455 (A)
D	$7,412 (F)	$8,900 (A)

49 P has the following budget and actual data:

Budget fixed overhead cost	$170,000
Budget production (units)	42,500
Actual fixed overhead cost	$182,000
Actual production (units)	40,000

The adverse fixed overhead volume variance is $_______

50 S has the following budget and actual data:

Budget fixed overhead cost	$1,248,480
Budget production (units)	20,400
Budgeted labour hours	104,040
Actual fixed overhead cost	$1,366,620
Actual production (units)	20,000
Actual labour hours	100,000

The favourable fixed overhead efficiency variance is $_______

The following data relate to Questions 51 and 52.

A hospital uses a standard costing system to monitor the performance of it surgeons. The following information is available for June:

The standard time to perform an eye operation is 2 hours. In June, the budget for eye operations showed that 320 operations would be performed and the (fixed) overheads attributable to eye operations would be $108,000.

The actual results showed that only 300 operations were performed in a total of 660 hours, and that the actual (fixed) overheads were $110,000.

---

51 **The fixed overhead capacity variance for June was:**

A $3,375 Adverse

B $3,375 Favourable

C $10,125 Favourable

D $10,125 Adverse

52 **The fixed overhead efficiency variance for June was:**

A $3,375 Adverse

B $3,375 Favourable

C $10,125 Favourable

D $10,125 Adverse

53 Trafalgar budgets to produce 10,000 units of product D12, each requiring 45 minutes of labour. Labour is charged at $20 per hour, and variable overheads at $15 per labour hour. During September, 11,000 units were produced. 8,000 hours of labour were paid at a total cost of $168,000. Variable overheads in September amounted to $132,000.

What is the variable overhead expenditure variance for September?

A $3,750 Favourable

B $6,125 Favourable

C $12,000 Adverse

D $12,000 Favourable

54 Trafalgar budgets to produce 10,000 units of product D12, each requiring 45 minutes of labour. Labour is charged at $20 per hour, and variable overheads at $15 per labour hour. During September, 11,000 units were produced. 8,000 hours of labour were paid at a total cost of $168,000. Variable overheads in September amounted to $132,000.

What is the labour efficiency variance for September?

A $5,000 Adverse

B $5,000 Favourable

C $5,250 Favourable

D $10,000 Adverse

55 Z sells PCs that it purchases through a regional distributor. An extract from its budget for the 4-week period ended 28 March 20X8 shows that it planned to sell 600 PCs at a unit price of $500, which would give a contribution to sales ratio of 25%.

Actual sales were 642 PCs at an average selling price of $465. The actual contribution to sales ratio averaged 20%.

What was the sales price variance (to the nearest $1)?

A $22,470 (F)

B $1,470 (A)

C $1,470 (F)

D $22,470 (A)

56 Z sells PCs that it purchases through a regional distributor. An extract from its budget for the 4-week period ended 28 March 20X8 shows that it planned to sell 600 PCs at a unit price of $500, which would give a contribution to sales ratio of 25%.

Actual sales were 642 PCs at an average selling price of $465. The actual contribution to sales ratio averaged 20%.

What was the sales volume contribution variance (to the nearest $1)?

A $5,050 (F)

B $5,150 (F)

C $5,250 (F)

D $5,350 (F)

57 **The fixed overhead volume variance is defined as:**

A the difference between the budgeted value of the fixed overheads and the standard fixed overheads absorbed by actual production

B the difference between the standard fixed overhead cost specified for the production achieved, and the actual fixed overhead cost incurred

C the difference between budgeted and actual fixed overhead expenditure

D the difference between the standard fixed overhead cost specified in the original budget and the same volume of fixed overheads, but at the actual prices incurred

58 Which of the following events would help to explain an adverse material usage variance *(place a tick for all those that apply)*?

		Correct?
(i)	The standard allowance for material wastage was set too high.	
(ii)	Material purchased was of a lower quality than standard.	
(iii)	Lower grade and less experienced employees were used than standard.	
(iv)	More material was purchased than budgeted for the period because output was higher than budgeted.	

59 A retailer uses an activity based budgeting system.

During the month of December it budgeted for $30,000 of inspection costs at a cost of $200 per inspection. Budgeted volume was 1,000 units. Actual results for December should inspection costs of $34,000 from 160 inspections. Actual volume was 1,200 units.

Using an activity based system, the favourable inspection efficiency variance for December is $_______

60 Which of the following is the most likely to result in an adverse variable overhead efficiency variance?

A Higher bonus payments to employees than standard

B Less experienced employees were used than standard

C The use of more expensive, higher quality materials than standard

D Machine power costs per hour were higher than standard

61 PQR Ltd operates a standard absorption costing system. Details of budgeted and actual figures are as follows:

	Budget	*Actual*
Sales volume (units)	100,000	110,000
Selling price per unit	$10	$9.50
Variable cost per unit	$5	$5.25
Total cost per unit	$8	$8.30

The favourable sales volume profit variance for the period was $_______

62 During a period, the staff of A worked 200 hours more than had been planned in the original budget, and 100 hours more than the standard time to produce the actual output. This would have caused which of the following variances.

A Favourable labour efficiency variance

B Adverse fixed overhead volume variance

C Favourable fixed overhead efficiency variance

D Favourable fixed overhead capacity variance

63 Q plc uses standard costing. The details for April were as follows:

Budgeted output	15,000	units
Budgeted labour hours	60,000	hours
Budgeted labour cost	$540,000	
Actual output	14,650	units
Actual labour hours paid	61,500	hours
Productive labour hours	56,000	hours
Actual labour cost	$522,750	

The idle time variance for April was $_______

64 **Match the variance with its most likely cause (draw a line connecting the variance to the correct cause)**

Variance
Material price variance
Material usage variance
Labour rate variance
Labour efficiency variance

Cause
Increased wastage due to a machine malfunction
Unexpected pay award
Increase in costs charged by a supplier
Improved operating procedures for staff.

65 **Which two of the following variances are most likely to be directly caused by purchasing better quality materials?**

	Caused by purchasing better quality?
Favourable fixed overhead expenditure variance	
Favourable material usage variance	
Adverse labour rate variance	
Favourable labour efficiency variance	
Favourable labour rate variance	

66 **Which of the following managers is most likely to be responsible for an adverse materials price variance?**

A Production manager

B Purchasing manager

C Human resources manager

D Finance manager

67 **Which of the following managers is most likely to be responsible for an adverse labour efficiency variance?**

A Production manager

B Purchasing manager

C Human resources manager

D Finance manager

68 **Which of the following variances would be affected if the company switched from an absorption costing system to a marginal costing system?**

	Affected?
Sales price variance	
Sales quantity profit variance	
Fixed overhead expenditure variance	
Fixed overhead capacity variance	

69 Annabelle uses activity based costing to allocate its overheads. The standard cost expected for the setups cost pool were:

Budgeted units	22,000
Budgeted setups	220
Budgeted cost	$6,820

The Actual costs incurred were

Actual units	21,000
Actual setups	200
Actual cost	$6,300

The expenditure variance for the setups was $______

70 A company produces two products with the following standard information:

	Product X	*Product Y*
Production and sales	*10,000 units*	*18,000 units*
Direct labour ($7 per hour)	$14.00	$10.50
Variable overhead	$3.00	$2.25

The company actually spent $87,140 on variable overheads, whilst labour worked for 46,000 hours. 12,000 units of X and 16,000 units of Y were produced.

The favourable variable overhead efficiency variance is $_______

71 Alderholt uses activity based costing to allocate its overheads. The following information is provided for the supervisor cost:

	Budget	*Actual*
Total employees	5,000	5,500
Number of supervisors	75	77
Supervisor cost	$7,500	$8,085

What was the total variance for the supervisor cost?

A $585 Adverse

B $165 Favourable

C $5550 Favourable

D $385 Adverse

72 An audit firm budgeted to provide 60 audits in the next month at a fee of $6,000 each. It actually made total sales of $365,400 from 58 audits.

To the nearest $, the favourable sales price variance is $______

73 A manufacturer has the following standard information for its audit services:

	$
Standard selling price	50
Standard contribution	20
Standard profit	15
Marginal cost	30

During the year it produced and sold 60,000 units. Budgeted production and sales was 65,000 units. The firm uses a marginal costing system for determining variances.

What will be the value of the adverse sales volume variance for the year?

A $75,000

B $100,000

C $150,000

D $250,000

74 A poster campaign was expected to create 25,000 posters using 6 metres of material per poster which costs $10 per metre.

The actual campaign had 20,000 posters using 122,000 metres of material at a total cost of $1,232,200.

The total adverse materials variance for the campaign was $______

75 A firm of architects provides standard building evaluations which require 4 hours of skilled labour paid at $60 per hour. During October, 500 evaluations were provided at a total labour cost of $120,900. 1,950 labour hours were used.

The adverse labour rate variance for October is $______

76 A manufacturer has the following standard cost per unit for labour:

	$
Direct labour(12 minutes)	10

In February the manufacturer spent $2.51m on 50,000 hours of labour. Actual production was 240,000 units.

What is the total labour variance for February?

A $10,000 Favourable

B $10,000 Adverse

C $110,000 Favourable

D $110,000 Adverse

FURTHER VARIANCE ANALYSIS

77 SS Ltd operates a standard marginal costing system. An extract from the standard cost card for the labour costs of one of its products is as follows:

Labour cost	
5 hours × $12	$60

Actual results for the period were as follows:

Production	11,500 units
Labour rate variance	$45,000 adverse
Labour efficiency variance	$30,000 adverse

The actual rate paid per direct labour hour for the period was $_______

78 During a period, Jones had the following budgeted and actual sales:

	Product A	*Product B*
Sales budget (units)	800	800
Actual sales (units)	750	700
Standard profit per unit	$5.00	$3.00

The total favourable sales mix profit variance for the period using the individual units method is $_______

79 During a period, A Ltd had the following budgeted and actual sales:

	Product A	*Product B*	*Product C*
Sales budget (units)	3,000	8,000	9,000
Actual sales (units)	4,000	7,500	11,500
Standard price per unit	$10.00	$8.00	$5.00
Actual price per unit	$9.50	$8.75	$4.00
Budgeted cost per unit	$8.00	$6.50	$3.20
Actual cost per unit	$8.00	$6.50	$3.20

The total favourable sales quantity profit variance for the period is $_______

80 PQ produces two products, Product B and Product C. The following budget and actual data relate to August:

	Product B	*Product C*
Budget data:		
Production and sales	2,200 units	1,800 units
Standard contribution per unit	$58.00	$59.75
Standard profit per unit	$50.00	$53.75
Actual data:		
Production and sales	3,000 units	1,500 units

The favourable sales mix profit variance for Product B is $______ *(use the individual units method)*

81 FF produces two products, Product R and Product S. The following budget and actual data was prepared for the period:

	Product R	*Product S*
Budget data:		
Production and sales	4,000 units	6,000 units
Standard contribution per unit	$6	$8
Standard profit per unit	$4	$3
Actual data:		
Production and sales	6,000 units	6,000 units

The sales quantity profit variance for Product S using the weighted average method is:

A $0

B $2,720

C $4,080

D $6,800

82 PP Ltd operates a standard absorption costing system. The following information has been extracted from the standard cost card for one of its products:

Budgeted production	1,500 units
Direct material cost: 7 kg × $4.10	$28.70 per unit
Actual results for the period were as follows:	
Production	1,600 units
Direct material (purchased and used): 12,000 kg	$52,200

It has subsequently been noted that, owing to a change in economic conditions, the best price that the material could have been purchased for was $4.50 per kg during the period.

The adverse material price planning variance was $______

83 The materials price variance for the month of January was $2,000 favourable and the usage variance was $450 favourable. The standard material usage per unit is 6 kg, and the standard material price is $3.00 per kg. 600 units were produced in the period and there was no change in inventory levels during the period.

Material purchases in the period were:

A 2,000 kg

B 2,933 kg

C 3,450 kg

D 3,600 kg

84 The following data relate to Product Z and its raw material content for September:

Budget	
Output	11,000 units of Z
Standard materials content	3 kg per unit at $4.00 per kg
Actual	
Output	10,000 units of Z
Materials purchased and used	32,000 kg at $4.80 per kg

It has now been agreed that the standard price for the raw material purchased in September should have been $5 per kg.

What was the materials operational price variance for September?

A $6,000 Adverse

B $6,400 Favourable

C $30,000 Adverse

D $32,000 Adverse

85 The following data relate to Product Z and its raw material content for September:

Budget	
Output	11,000 units of Z
Standard materials content	3 kg per unit at $4.00 per kg
Actual	
Output	10,000 units of Z
Materials purchased and used	32,000 kg at $4.80 per kg

It has now been agreed that the standard price for the raw material purchased in September should have been $5 per kg.

Using actual units produced, what was the materials planning price variance for September?

A $6,000 Adverse

B $30,000 Adverse

C $32,000 Adverse

D $33,000 Adverse

86 During a period, Jones had the following budgeted and actual sales:

	Product A	*Product B*
Sales budget (units)	800	800
Actual sales (units)	750	700
Standard profit per unit	$5.00	$3.00

The total adverse sales quantity profit variance for the period is $_______

87 The following data relate to Product Z and its raw material content for September:

Budget	
Output	11,000 units of Z
Standard materials content	3 kg per unit at $4.00 per kg
Actual	
Output	10,000 units of Z
Materials purchased and used	32,000 kg at $4.80 per kg

It has now been agreed that the standard price for the raw material purchased in September should have been $5 per kg.

What was the materials operational usage variance for September?

A $8,000 Adverse

B $9,600 Adverse

C $9,600 Favourable

D $10,000 Adverse

88 PP Ltd operates a standard absorption costing system. The following information has been extracted from the standard cost card for one of its products:

Budgeted production	1,500 units
Direct material cost: 7 kg × $4.10	$28.70 per unit
Actual results for the period were as follows:	
Production	1,600 units
Direct material (purchased and used): 12,000 kg	$52,200

It has subsequently been noted that, owing to a change in economic conditions, the best price that the material could have been purchased for was $4.50 per kg during the period.

The adverse operational material usage variance was $______

89 A museum has a new temporary exhibition for which it has budgeted for the following sales:

	Full Price Tickets	*Concessions*
Volume	9,000	3,000
Contribution per unit	$9	$4

Actual sales were as follows:

	Full Price Tickets	*Concessions*
Volume	12,000	8,000
Contribution per unit	$9	$5

To the nearest $, using the individual units method the favourable sales mix variance for concessions for the exhibition is $______

90 During a period, A Ltd had the following budgeted and actual sales:

	Product A	*Product B*	*Product C*
Sales budget (units)	3,000	8,000	9,000
Actual sales (units)	4,000	7,500	11,500
Standard price per unit	$10.00	$8.00	$5.00
Actual price per unit	$9.50	$8.75	$4.00
Budgeted cost per unit	$8.00	$6.50	$3.20
Actual cost per unit	$8.00	$6.50	$3.20

The total favourable sales mix profit variance for the period using the individual units method is $_______

91 Operation B, in a factory, has a standard time of 15 minutes. The standard rate of pay for operatives is $10 per hour. The budget for a period was based on carrying out the operation 350 times. It was subsequently realised that the standard time for Operation B included in the budget did not incorporate expected time savings from the use of new machinery from the start of the period. The standard time should have been reduced to 12 minutes.

Operation B was actually carried out 370 times in the period in a total of 80 hours. The operatives were paid $850.

The operational labour efficiency variance was:

A $60 adverse

B $75 favourable

C $100 adverse

D $125 adverse

92 A company operates a standard absorption costing system. The following fixed production overhead data are available for the latest period:

Budgeted output	300,000 units
Budgeted fixed production overhead	$1,500,000
Actual fixed production overhead	$1,950,000
Fixed production overhead total variance	$150,000 adverse

The actual level of production for the period was _______ units *(round to the nearest 1,000 units)*

93 A firm budgeted for material costs of $54,000 in May. Material was expected to cost $6 per kg each unit was expected to use 2 kg of material.

The actual cost of material in May was $56,000 and there was a favourable material price variance of $4,220.

The actual quantity of materials purchased in May was _______ kg

BUDGETING AND BUDGETARY CONTROL

PREPARING BUDGETS

94 Which of the following can be identified as purposes of budgeting (*tick all that apply*)?

	Purpose of budgeting?
Communication	
Authorisation	
Sales maximisation	
Co-ordination	

95 Which of the following statements regarding budgeting is NOT true?

A Functional budgets should be prepared before the master budget

B The cash budget is not part of the master budget

C Functional budgeting should start with the budget for the principal budget factor

D The production budget is needed before the material usage budget can be prepared

96 A manufacturer sells its sole product at $200 per unit. It has the following budgeted sales for the next three quarters:

Quarter	1	2	3
Sales ($000)	500	600	800

It has a policy of maintaining inventory at 10% of the following month's sales volume.

What is the number of units to be produced in quarter 2?

A 620 units

B 2,900 units

C 3,000 units

D 3,100 units

97 PP Ltd is preparing the production and material purchases budgets for one of their products, the SUPERX, for the forthcoming year.

The following information is available:

Sales demand (units)	30,000
Material usage per unit	7 kgs
Estimated opening inventory	3,500 units
Required closing inventory	35% higher than opening inventory

How many units of the SUPERX will need to be produced?

A 28,775

B 30,000

C 31,225

D 38,225

98 Which of the following is not a typical problem that organisations may face when dealing with big data?

A The increasing use of electronic devices within society at large

B A lack of skills in the labour pool relating to the handling of Big Data

C Legal and privacy issues if data is held about individuals

D Measurement of metrics that have no use to the organisation

99 EFG uses an Activity Based Budgeting system. It manufactures three products, budgeted details of which are set out below:

	Product E	*Product F*	*Product G*
Budgeted annual production (units)	75,000	120,000	60,000
Batch size (units)	200	60	30
Machine set-ups per batch	5	3	9

Three cost pools have been identified. Budgeted machine set-up costs for the year are $180,000.

The budgeted machine set-up cost per unit of product F is $______

100 An incremental budgeting system is:

A a system which budgets only for the extra costs associated with a particular plan

B a system which budgets for the variable manufacturing costs only

C a system which prepares budgets only after the manager responsible has justified the continuation of the relevant activity

D a system which prepares budgets by adjusting the previous year's values by expected changes in volumes of activity and price/inflation effects

101 A company has the following expected sales for the next three months of the year:

April	12,000 units
May	15,000 units
June	18,000 units

The opening inventory of the product in April is expected to be 3,600 units.

At the end of each month closing inventory is expected to equal 30% of the following month's sales.

The expected level of production in May is ______ units

102 Which of the following is a common feature of a beyond budgeting approach?

A A greater use of rolling budgets

B A greater use of top-down budgets

C A greater emphasis on financial targets

D A greater focus on standardisation

103 Which of the following definitions best describes 'Zero-Based Budgeting'?

A A method of budgeting where an attempt is made to make the expenditure under each cost heading as close to zero as possible.

B A method of budgeting whereby all activities are re-evaluated each time a budget is formulated.

C A method of budgeting that recognises the difference between the behaviour of fixed and variable costs with respect to changes in output and the budget is designed to change appropriately with such fluctuations.

D A method of budgeting where the sum of revenues and expenditures in each budget centre must equal zero.

104 Nile is preparing its sales budget . Estimated sales are 120,000 units if the Summer is rainy, and 80,000 units if the Summer is dry. The probability of a dry Summer is 0.4.

What is the expected value for sales volume?

A 96,000 units

B 100,000 units

C 104,000 units

D 120,000 units

1055 Identify which of the following statements about Big Data are true or false?

	True	False
Big Data management involves using sophisticated systems to gather, store and analyse large volumes of data		
Data can be a variety of structured and unstructured formats.		
Big data does not include traditional data from internal sources such as sales history, preferences, order frequency and pricing information.		
Big Data does include information from external sources such as websites, trade publications and social networks.		

106 MM is preparing its cash budget for February using the following data.

One line in the cash budget is for purchases of a raw material, J. The opening inventory of J in January is expected to be 1,075 units. The price of J is expected to be $8 per unit. The company pays for purchases at the end of the month following delivery.

Production is expected to be 4,300 units in January and 5,300 units in February and each production unit uses one unit of material J.

At the end of each month raw materials inventory is expected to be 25% of the requirement for the following month's production.

The value for purchases of J to be included in the cash budget for February is $_______

107 K has determined a cost driver rate for quality testing as $850 per test.

During the year there were actually on average 50 tests per month, giving an adverse variance on the total cost for quality testing of $102,000 for the year.

The budgeted cost per month for quality testing is $_______

108 A master budget comprises the:

A budgeted income statement and budgeted cash flow only

B budgeted income statement and budgeted balance sheet only

C budgeted income statement and budgeted capital expenditure only

D budgeted income statement, budgeted balance sheet and budgeted cash flow only

109 D plc operates a retail business. Purchases are sold at cost plus 25%. The management team is preparing the cash budget and has gathered the following data:

1 The budgeted sales are as follows:

Month	$000
July	100
August	90
September	125

2 It is management policy to hold inventory at the end of each month which is sufficient to meet sales demand in the next half month. Sales are budgeted to occur evenly during each month.

3 Creditors are paid one month after the purchase has been made.

The entry for 'purchases' that will be shown in the cash budget for August is $_____

110 A company has the following budgeted sales figures:

Month 1	$105,000
Month 2	$120,000
Month 3	$108,000

80% of sales are on credit and the remainder are paid in cash. Credit customers paying within one month are given a discount of 1.5%. Credit customers normally pay within the following time frame:

Within 1 month	40% of credit sales
Within 2 months	98% of credit sales

There is an expectation that 2% of credit sales will become irrecoverable (bad) debts.

Outstanding receivables at the beginning of month 1 includes $6,000 expected to be received in month 3.

The total receipts expected in month 3 are $_______

111 CJD Ltd manufactures plastic components for the car industry. The following budgeted information is available for three of its key plastic components:

	W	*X*	*Y*
	$ per unit	$ per unit	$ per unit
Selling price	200	183	175
Direct material	50	40	35
Direct labour	30	35	30
Units produced and sold	10,000	15,000	18,000

The total number of activities for each of the three products for the period is as follows:

Number of purchase requisitions	1,200	1,800	2,000
Number of set ups	240	260	300

Overhead costs have been analysed as follows:

Receiving/inspecting quality assurance	$1,400,000
Production scheduling/machine set up	$1,200,000

The budgeted profit per unit for Product X using activity-based budgeting is $______

112 GS has budgeted sales for the next two years of 24,000 units per annum spread evenly throughout both years. The estimated opening inventory of finished goods at the start of the next year is 500 units but GS now wants to maintain inventory of finished goods equivalent to one month's sales.

Each unit uses 2 kg of material. The estimated opening raw material inventory at the start of the next year is 300 kg but GS now wants to hold sufficient raw material inventory at the end of each month to cover the following month's production.

The change in the policy for inventory holding for both raw materials and finished goods will take effect in the first month of next year and will apply for the next two years.

The budgeted material cost is $12 per kg.

The material purchases budget for the next year is $______

113 JB has budgeted production for the next budget year of 36,000 units. Each unit of production requires 4 labour hours and the budgeted labour rate is $12 per hour excluding overtime. Idle time is expected to be 10% of total hours available i.e. including idle time. Due to labour shortages it is expected that 20% of the hours paid, including idle time, will be paid at an overtime rate of time and a half.

The labour cost budget for the year is $______

114 B's latest estimate for trade payables outstanding at the end of this year is 45 days. Estimated purchases for this year are $474,500. DB is preparing the budget for next year and estimates that purchases will increase by 10%.

The trade payables amount, in $, outstanding at the end of next year is estimated to be the same as at the end of this year.

The budgeted trade payable days at the end of next year are ______ days *(round to the nearest whole day)*

115 AB is preparing its cash budget for next year. The accounts receivable at the beginning of next year are expected to be $460,000. The budgeted sales are $5,400,000 and will occur evenly throughout the year. 80% of the budgeted sales will be on credit and the remainder will be cash sales. Credit customers pay in the month following sale.

The budgeted cash receipts from customers next year are:

A $5,040,000

B $5,410,000

C $5,500,000

D $5,890,000

116 AB is preparing its purchases budget for raw material C for the forthcoming year. The opening inventory of raw material C is expected to be 2,000 kg and the price is expected to be $8 per kg.

Raw material C is used only in the production of Product D. Each unit of Product D requires two kg of material C. Budgeted sales of Product D for the forthcoming year and for the following year are 36,000 units in each year. Sales will occur evenly throughout each year. The opening inventory is expected to be 6,000 units.

AB will implement a new inventory policy from the first month of the forthcoming year. The closing inventory that will be required at the end of the forthcoming year is as follows:

Raw material inventory: one month's production requirements

Finished goods inventory: one month's sales requirements

The material purchases budget for the forthcoming year is $_______

117 PJ has budgeted sales for the next two years of 144,000 units per annum spread evenly throughout each year. The estimated closing inventory at the end of this year is 6,500 units. PJ wants to change its inventory policy so that it holds inventory equivalent to one month's sales. The change in inventory policy will take place at the beginning of next year and will apply for the next two years.

Each unit produced requires 2 hours of direct labour. The budgeted direct labour rate per hour is $15. It is anticipated that 80% of production will be paid at the budgeted rate and the remainder will be paid at the overtime rate of time and a half. PJ treats overtime costs as part of direct labour costs.

The direct labour cost budget for the next year is $_______

118 Big data can be difficult to manage for a variety of reasons. These can be summarised using the 3 V's.

Which of the following correctly describes volume?

A The speed at which data is generated

B The quantity of the data that is generated

C The range of data that is generated

D The accuracy of the data that is generated

119 Match the following costs to the correct budget (draw a line connecting the cost to the correct budget)

Cost
Commission paid to an agent for selling the product
Electricity used in the factory
Depreciation of factory building
Packaging material to protect the product

Budget
Distribution overhead budget
Variable production overhead budget
Selling overhead budget
Fixed production overhead budget

120 D plc operates a retail business. Purchases are sold at cost plus 25%. The management team is preparing the cash budget and has gathered the following data:

1 The budgeted sales are as follows:

Month	$000
August	90
September	125
October	140

2 It is management policy to hold inventory at the end of each month which is sufficient to meet sales demand in the next half month. Sales are budgeted to occur evenly during each month.

3 Creditors are paid one month after the purchase has been made.

The entry for 'purchases' that will be shown in the cash budget for September is $_____

121 AB is preparing its cash budget for next year. The estimated accounts payable balance at the beginning of next year is $540,000. The budgeted purchases for next year are $6,800,000, occurring evenly throughout the year. It is estimated that 75% of purchases will be on credit and the remainder will be for cash. The company pays for credit purchases in the month following purchase.

The budgeted cash payments to suppliers next year are:

A $6,375,000

B $6,773,333

C $6,915,000

D $5,215,000

122 Which of the following would be included in the fixed production overhead budget?

A The annual salary of a supervisor that monitors the performance of factory workers

B The annual rent charged on the head office building

C The annual variable electricity usage charge of the factory machinery used to make the product

D The annual cost of materials used to make the product

123 The following costs have been estimated for the following period.

Direct material	$20,000
Electricity	$8,750
Indirect labour	$37,500
Rent	$6,000
Royalty fee	$2,150

What would be the total overhead budget for the period?

A $74,000

B $72,250

C $52,250

D $14,750

124 During a period, A Ltd expected to produce 5,000 units using 16,000 labour hours and 9,000 machine hours.

If the budgeted overhead absorption rate was $12.50 per labour hour, the budgeted fixed overheads in the period were $_______

125 The following budgeted information comes from the accounting records of ABC

	Product A	*Product B*
Production units	1,000	2,000
Labour hours per unit	0.5 hours	2 hours
Machine hours per unit	0.25 hours	1.5 hours
Variable overhead rate (per machine hour)	$1.50 per hour	
Fixed overhead rate (per labour hour)	$1.95 per hour	

What would be the total overhead budget for the period?

A $11,625

B $13,088

C $13,650

D $15,113

126 **Which TWO of the following are not criticisms of incremental budgeting?**

	Not a criticism?
It may make managers, staff and unions feel threatened	
It encourages slack	
It is time consuming as it involves starting from scratch	
It encourages wasteful spending	
It includes past inefficiencies as costs are not scrutinised	

127 Which two of the following are not characteristics of rolling budgets?

	Characteristic of rolling budgets?
Budgets are more likely to be realistic as there is a shorter period between preparation and actual events occurring	
Updates to budgets are only made when they are foreseeable	
They reduce uncertainty in budgeting	
They force management to look ahead more frequently	
Each item of expenditure must be fully justified before inclusion in the budget	

128 Which one of the following best describes incremental budgeting?

A Increments of income and expenditure are compared with forecasted results

B A method of budgeting where all activities are re-evaluated each time a budget is formulated

C A budget updated in regular increments by adding a further accounting period when the earliest period has expired

D The budget for each period is based on prior period results, modified for changes in activity levels

129 The following is a description of which method of budgeting?

'A budget continuously updated by adding a further accounting period when the earliest accounting period has expired.'

A Zero based budgeting

B Activity based budgeting

C Incremental budgeting

D Rolling budgets

130 LF has the following expected production for the next three months:

Month	*1*	*2*	*3*
	units	*units*	*units*
Production	1,850	1,800	2,020

The variable production overhead cost per unit is $1.20. 60% of these will be paid in the month in which production occurs and the remainder will be paid one month later.

What will be the variable overhead payment in month 2?

A $2,160

B $2,424

C $1,296

D $2,184

131 RF has prepared the following sales forecast for its first three months of trading:

Month	*Number of components*
1	1,500
2	1,750
3	2,000

The selling price has been set at $10 per component in the first three months.

Sales receipts

Time of payment	% of customers
Month of sale	20*
One month later	45
Two months later	25
Three months later	5

The balance represents anticipated bad debts.

*A 2% discount is given to customers for payment received in the month of sale.

The sales receipts for month 2 are budgeted to be $_______

132 **Which of the following best describes Zero Based Budgeting (ZBB)?**

A A method of budgeting where all activities are re-evaluated each time a budget is formulated

B A method of budgeting that tries to make expenditure as close to zero as possible

C method of budgeting where the sum of all costs and revenues must be zero

D A budget that has zero variance between forecast and actual results

FORECASTING

133 The following details relate to product X in two accounting periods:

Number of units	500	800
	$/unit	$/unit
Direct materials	2.00	2.00
Direct labour	1.50	1.50
Production overhead	2.50	1.75
Other overhead	1.00	0.625
	7.00	5.875

The fixed cost per period and variable cost per unit are:

	Period fixed cost	*Variable cost/unit*
	$	$
A	1,000	1.125
B	1,000	4.00
C	1,500	3.50
D	1,500	4.00

134 A company is estimating future sales using time series analysis. The following trend equation has been derived from actual sales data for Year 1:

$$y = 22{,}000 + 800x$$

where y is the total sales units for the quarter, and

x is the time period (Quarter 1 of Year 1 is time period 1)

The following set of seasonal variations have been derived based on Year 1 actual sales:

Quarter 1	–7,080
Quarter 2	–2,360
Quarter 3	+7,080
Quarter 4	–2,360

What would be the forecast sales for the amount of the seasonal variation for Year 2, Quarter 3?

A 19,720 units

B 20,520 units

C 33,880 units

D 34,680 units

135 XYZ Ltd is preparing the production budget for the next period. The total costs of production are a semi-variable cost. The following cost information has been collected in connection with production:

Volume (units)	*Cost*
4,500	$29,000
6,500	$33,000

The estimated total production costs for a production volume of 5,750 units is nearest to

A $29,200

B $30,000

C $31,500

D $32,500

136 The following cost per unit details have been extracted from a production overhead cost budget:

Output (units)	6,000	10,000
Production overhead ($/unit)	3.20	3.00

The budget cost allowance for production overhead for an activity level of 7,350 units is:

A $20,505

B $21,765

C $22,845

D $23,515

137 A company is estimating its costs based on past information. The total costs incurred by the company at different levels of output were as follows:

Output (units)	*Total costs* $
160,000	2,420,000
185,000	2,775,000
190,000	2,840,000

The company uses the high-low method to separate total costs into their fixed and variable elements. Ignore inflation.

What is the estimated total costs for an output of 205,000 units?

A $2,870,000

B $3,050,000

C $3,064,211

D $3,080,857

138 The overhead costs of RP have been found to be accurately represented by the formula:

y = $10,000 + $0.25x

where y is the monthly cost and x represents the activity level measured as the number of orders.

Monthly activity levels of orders may be estimated using a combined regression analysis and time series model:

a = 100,000 + 30b

where a represents the de-seasonalised monthly activity level and b represents the month number.

In month 240, the seasonal index value is 108.

The overhead cost for RP for month 240 is $_______ *(round to the nearest $1,000)*

139 Monthly sales of product R follow a linear trend of y = 9.72 + 5.816x, where y is the number of units sold and x is the number of the month. Monthly deviations from the trend follow an additive model.

The forecast number of units of product R to be sold in month 23, which has a seasonal factor of plus 6.5 is, to the nearest whole unit:

A 134

B 137

C 143

D 150

140 The budgeted total costs for two levels of output are as shown below:

Output	25,000 units	40,000 units
Total cost	$143,500	$194,000

Within this range of output it is known that the variable cost per unit is constant but fixed costs rise by $10,000 when output exceeds 35,000 units.

The total fixed costs for a budgeted output of 36,000 units are $______

141 A company is preparing its maintenance budget. The number of machine hours and maintenance costs for the past six months have been as follows:

Month	*Machine hours*	$
1	10,364	35,319
2	12,212	39,477
3	8,631	31,420
4	9,460	33,285
5	8,480	31,080
6	10,126	34,784

The budget cost allowance for an activity level of 9,340 machine hours, before any adjustment for price changes, is nearest to:

A $21,000

B $30,200

C $33,000

D $34,000

142 A company is preparing its annual budget and is estimating the number of units of Product A that it will sell in each quarter of Year 2. Past experience has shown that the trend for sales of the product is represented by the following relationship:

y = a + bx where

y = number of sales units in the quarter

a = 10,000 units

b = 3,000 units

x = the quarter number where 1 = quarter 1 of Year 1

Actual sales of Product A in Year 1 were affected by seasonal variations and were as follows:

Quarter 1: 14,000 units

Quarter 2: 18,000 units

Quarter 3: 18,000 units

Quarter 4: 20,000 units

After adjusting for seasonal variations, the expected sales of Product A for Quarter 3 of Year 2 is ______ units

143 The following budgeted information comes from the accounting records of Ross

Production units	*1,000*	*2,000*	*3,000*
	$	$	$
Material cost	15,000	30,000	45,000
Labour cost	10,000	20,000	30,000
Overhead cost	18,000	22,000	26,000
Distribution cost	12,000	12,000	12,000
Total cost	55,000	84,000	113,000

What would be the budgeted cost for 2,750 units?

A $103,583

B $105,750

C $106,750

D $109,250

144 A company is estimating its costs based on past information. The total costs incurred by the company at different levels of output were as follows:

Output (units)	*Total costs ($)*
160,000	2,420,000
185,000	2,775,000
190,000	2,840,000

The company uses the high-low method to separate total costs into their fixed and variable elements. Ignore inflation. The company has now established that there is a stepped increase in fixed costs of $30,000 when output reaches 180,000 units.

What is the estimate of total costs for an output of 175,000 units?

A $2,645,000

B $2,275,000

C $2,615,000

D $2,630,000

145 A company has calculated that the coefficient of determination between output and production costs over a number of months is 89%.

Which TWO of the following comments are correct?

	Correct?
89% of the variation in production costs from one month to the next can be explained by corresponding variation in output.	
Costs increase as output increases.	
The linear relationship between output and costs is very strong.	
An increase of 100% in output is associated with an increase of 89% in costs.	
An increase of 89% in output is associated with an increase of 100% in costs.	

146 The following budgeted information comes from the accounting records of Ross Ltd

Production units	1,000	2,000
Budgeted cost	$18,000	$24,000

What would be the budgeted cost for 1,980 units?

A $19,680

B $21,480

C $23,880

D $24,280

BUDGETARY CONTROL

147 Which two of the following are limitations of 'what if' analysis in cash budgeting?

	Limitations of 'What if' analysis?
Only one variable changes at a time	
It assesses the risk to the closing cash balance	
It provides an assessment of how responsive the cash flows are to changes in variables	
Probabilities of changes are not accounted for	
It directs attention to critical variables	

148 A retailer has prepared the following budget for one country where it operates in 20 locations:

	$000
Revenue	6,800
Cost of sales	4,500
Other operating costs	1,600
Net profit	700

The retailer wants to test what impact would be seen on profit if revenue was to fall by 40%. It expects that it would save $400,000 on rent by closing stores but would have to pay $250,000 in redundancy costs to affected staff. Cost of sales are believed to be 80% variable and 20% fixed.

What would be the fall in profit for the year?

A $430

B $1,170

C $1,130

D $1,870

149 Which of the following best describes 'budgetary slack'?

A The difference between what has been set as a budgetary objective and what has been achieved for the period

B The demotivating impact of a budgetary target that has been set too high

C The deliberate over-estimation of expenditure and/or under-estimation of revenues in the budgetary planning process

D Accumulated favourable variances reported against a specific item of budgeted expenditure

150 Murray had the following budget and actual results during a period:

	Original budget	*Actual*
Sales units	1,000	1,380
	$	$
Sales revenue	100,000	133,860
Direct material	40,000	57,800
Direct labour	20,000	27,000
Variable overhead	15,000	18,600
Fixed overhead	10,000	11,000
Profit	15,000	19,460

Using a flexed budget approach, the total adverse profit variance for the period is $_______

151 A flexible budget is best defined as

A A budget for a single level of activity that does not change in a period

B A budget that is based on zero expenditure and is only increased if the expenditure is fully justified

C A budget for the number of units that were actually sold during a period

D A budget that can be restated to any level of output

152 X Co uses rolling budgeting, updating its budgets on a quarterly basis. After carrying out the last quarter's update to the cash budget, it projected a forecast cash deficit of $400,000 at the end of the year. Consequently, the planned purchase of new capital equipment has been postponed.

Which of the following types of control is the sales manager's actions an example of?

A Feedforward control

B Negative feedback control

C Positive feedback control

D Double loop feedback control

153 The following budgeted information comes from the accounting records of Smith

	Original budget
Sales units	1,000
	$
Sales revenue	100,000
Direct material	40,000
Direct labour	20,000
Variable overhead	15,000
Fixed overhead	10,000
Profit	15,000

In a period where the actual sales were 1,200 units, what would be the flexed budget?

A $17,000

B $20,000

C $22,000

D $35,000

154 What is the purpose of a flexible budget?

A To compare actual and budgeted results at virtually any level of production

B To reduce the total time in preparing the annual budget

C To allow management some latitude in meeting goals

D To eliminate cyclical fluctuations in production reports by ignoring variable costs

155 Which of the following is an advantage of non-participative budgeting as compared to participative budgeting?

A It increases motivation

B It is less time consuming

C It increases acceptance

D The budgets produced are more attainable

156 Which of the following is not an impact caused by unethical behaviour in the budgeting system?

A Damage to an organisation's share price caused by over-stating actual results

B Damage to an organisation's reputation due to poor treatment of budget holders

C Budget holders encouraging staff to ignore unattainable budget targets

D Budget holders using aggressive policies to achieve targeted results

157 A law firm has forecast its cash balances for the next six months as follows:

Month	*1*	*2*	*3*	*4*	*5*	*6*
	$000	$000	$000	$000	$000	$000
Net cash flow	80	120	(250)	(260)	400	320
Opening cash balance	200	280	400	150	(110)	290
Closing cash balance	280	400	150	(110)	290	610

Staff are paid in the month that they perform work. The firm have taken on a new client where work will be performed in month 3 and the customer is expected to pay their $300,000 invoice in month 4. This work is invoiced at a 50% mark up on labour costs (the only directly attributable cost for the client work).

The firm have an overdraft limit of $250,000 and want to test whether the limit will be breached if the customer fails to pay for the work performed.

If the customer does not pay their invoice by how much will the overdraft be exceeded in month 4?

A $0

B $110,000

C $160,000

D $410,000

158 A retailer has forecast receipts for the its first three months of operations as follows:

Month	*Jan*	*Feb*	*March*
Sales (Units × $40)	60,000	70,000	40,000
Paid in month – 20% × 0.95	11,400	13,300	7,600
50% in the following month		30,000	35,000
30% in 3rd month			18,000
Receipts	11,400	43,300	60,600

Customers who pay in the month of sales will receive a 5% settlement discount. As part of the retailer's sensitivity analysis it wants to examine the impact on receipts if only 15% of customers pay in the month of sales (with 55% of customers paying in the month following the sale.

The revised cash receipts in March would be $_______

159 **Consider whether following statement regarding feed-forward control budgetary systems are true or false:**

	True	False
Feed-forward control systems have an advantage over other types of control in that it establishes how effective planning was.		
Feed-forward control occurs while an activity is in progress.		

160 A manufacturer has prepared a production budget for the next three months (based on the new assumption that closing inventory would be 20% of the next month's sales) as follows:

Production budget (units)	*June*	*July*	*August*
Sales	14,000	9,000	12,000
Add closing inventory	1,800	2,400	3,000
Less opening inventory	3,600	1,800	2,400
Production	12,200	9,600	12,600

The manufacturer wants to perform some sensitivity analysis on the basis that the inventory level is reduced to 10% of the following month's sales.

The new budgeted production in July would be ______ units.

SHORT-TERM COMMERCIAL DECISION MAKING

RELEVANT COSTS AND DECISION MAKING

161 An organisation is considering the costs to be incurred in respect of a special order opportunity.

The order would require 1,250 kgs of material D. This is a material that is readily available and regularly used by the organisation on its normal products. There are 265 kgs of material D in stock which cost $795 last week. The current market price is $3.24 per kg.

Material D is normally used to make product X. Each unit of X requires 3 kgs of material D, and if material D is costed at $3 per kg, each unit of X yields a contribution of $15.

What is the relevant cost of material D to be included in the costing of the special order?

A $3,990

B $4,050

C $10,000

D $10,300

162 H Ltd has in stock 15,000 kg of M, a raw material which it bought for $3/kg five years ago, for a product line which was discontinued four years ago.

At present, M has no use in its existing state but could be sold as scrap for $1.00 per kg. One of the company's current products (HN) requires 4 kg of a raw material which is available for $5.00 per kg. M can be modified at a cost of $0.75 per kg so that it may be used as a substitute for this material. However, after modification, 5 kg of M is required for every unit of HN to be produced.

H Ltd has now received an invitation to tender for a product which could use M in its present state.

What is the relevant cost per kg of M to be included in the cost estimate for the tender?

A $0.75

B $1.00

C $3.00

D $3.25

163 UU Company has been asked to quote for a special contract which will require material X. The following information is available on material X:

Book value	Scrap value	Replacement cost
$5.00 per kg	$0.50 per kg	$5.50 per kg

The special contract would require 10 kgs of Material X. There are 250 kgs of this material in stock which was purchased in error over two years ago. It has just been noticed that if Material X is modified, at a cost of $2 per kg, it could then be used as a substitute for material Y which is in regular use and currently costs $6 per kg.

The relevant cost of the materials for the special contract is:

A $5

B $40

C $50

D $55

164 A company has been asked to quote for a special contract. The following information is available on the labour required for the contract:

The special contract would require 100 hours of labour. However, the labourers, who are each paid $15 per hour, are working at full capacity. There is a shortage of labour in the market and therefore the labour required to undertake this special contract would have to be taken from another contract, Z, which currently utilises 500 hours of labour and generates $5,000 worth of contribution. If the labour was taken from contract Z, then the whole of contract Z would have to be delayed, and such delay would invoke a penalty fee of $1,000.

What is the relevant cost of labour?

A $1,000

B $1,500

C $2,500

D $7,500

165 A company is preparing a quotation for a one-month consultancy project. Currently the company employs a consultant on an annual salary of $36,000.

This consultant is fully employed on current projects and, if she were to be transferred to this new project, then an existing junior consultant would be used to cover her current work. The junior consultant would be paid a bonus of $5,000 for undertaking this additional responsibility.

Alternatively the company could hire an external consultant on a one month contract at a cost of $4,500.

The relevant cost to be used in preparing the quotation is:

A $4,500

B $5,000

C $40,500

D $41,000

166 Jones Company is bidding for a contract which is due to be started within a few days. The contract will use up its stock of Material XY which will otherwise be held for one month. In one month's time, there is a probability of 0.6 that it will be used. If it is not used then the material will be sold. Estimates are as follows:

	$
Replacement cost of stock in one month's time	15,000
Sales value in one month's time	12,000
Stock holding cost for one month	900

The expected relevant cost of Material XY for use when evaluating the viability of the contract is $_______

167 In order to utilise some spare capacity, K Ltd is preparing a quotation for a special order which requires 2,000 kgs of material J.

K Ltd has 800 kgs of material J in stock (original cost $7.00 per kg). Material J is used in the company's main product L. Each unit of L uses 5 kgs of material J and, based on an input value of $7.00 per kg of J, each unit of L yields a contribution of $10.00.

The resale value of material J is $5.50 per kg. The present replacement price of material J is $8.00 per kg. Material J is readily available in the market.

The relevant cost of the 2,000 kgs of material J to be included in the quotation is $_______

168 **Which of the following statements is NOT an advantage of acting ethically in business decision making?**

A The organisation will become more attractive to stakeholders

B Global organisations can have a consistent global approach to decision making

C Business risk can be reduced

D The risk of regulatory breaches is reduced

169 A company is calculating the relevant cost of the material to be used on a particular contract.

The contract requires 4,200 kgs of material H and this can be bought for $6.30 per kg.

The company bought 10,000 kgs of material H some time ago when it paid $4.50 per kg. Currently 3,700 kgs of this remains in stock. The stock of material H could be sold for $3.20 per kg.

The company has no other use for material H other than on this contract, but it could modify it at a cost of $3.70 per kg and use it as a substitute for material J. Material J is regularly used by the company and can be bought for $7.50 per kg.

The relevant cost of the material for the contract is:

A $17,210

B $19,800

C $26,460

D $30,900

170 A company manufactures two joint products and a by-product in a single process, which are all sold as soon as they are output from the process, without further processing. Joint costs are shared on the basis of sales value at the split-off point and the revenue from the by-product is credited to the cost of production.

The budget for the next period is as follows:

Processing costs: $45,000

Output in units:

Joint product X – 250 units

Joint product Y – 400 units

By-product Z – 3,000 units

Selling prices per unit: $80 for X, $100 for Y, $0.20 for Z.

The cost per unit of product Y is $_______

171 P Limited is considering whether to continue making a component or buy it from an outside supplier. It uses 12,000 of the components each year.

The internal manufacturing cost comprises:

	$/unit
Direct materials	3.00
Direct labour	4.00
Variable overhead	1.00
Specific fixed cost	2.50
Other fixed costs	2.00
	12.50

If the direct labour were not used to manufacture the component, it would be used to increase the production of another item for which there is unlimited demand. This other item has a contribution of $10.00 per unit but requires $8.00 of labour per unit.

The maximum price per component at which buying is preferable to internal manufacture is:

A $8.00

B $10.50

C $12.50

D $15.50

172 A company manufactures a range of products one of which, product L, incurs a total cost of $60 per unit.

The company manufactures 50,000 units each year and the directors wish to achieve a return of 20% on the total capital of $10,000,000 invested in the company.

Based on this information the cost-plus selling price (to the nearest $) of one unit of product L should be $_____

173 Which of the following accounting entries is ignored when making decisions based on relevant costs and revenues?

A Increases to pension cost provisions

B Reductions in loans

C Increases in non-current assets

D Reductions in working capital

174 JK manufactures a product with the following standard information:

	$/unit
Direct materials	9.00
Direct labour	14.00
Total direct cost	23.00

Additional information on the product is provided as follows:

Direct labour hours per unit	2 hours
Production overhead absorption rate	$4.50 per direct labour hour
Mark-up for non-production overhead costs	10% of total production costs
Required return on sales revenue	20%

The target selling price for the product will be:

A $27.60

B $40.00

C $42.24

D $44.00

175 A factory's entire machine capacity is used to produce essential components. The costs of using the machines are as follows:

	$
Variable costs	15,000
Fixed costs	50,000
	65,000

If all the components are purchased from an outside supplier, the machines could be used to produce other items which would earn a total contribution of $25,000.

The maximum price that a profit-maximising company should be willing to pay to the outside supplier for the components is $_______

176 The standard output from a joint process was 5,000 litres of Product K, 3,000 litres of Product L and 2,000 litres of Product M. The total cost of the joint process was $156,000. The company is now deciding if it should modify Product K by putting it through an additional process.

In order to help with that decision the best way to apportion the joint costs of $156,000 to the products is:

A in the ratio of 5 : 3 : 2

B in the ratio of the sales value at the split off point

C in the ratio of the sales value after further processing

D none of the above method

177 Which of the following costs would not be treated as a relevant cost when making a decision on a potential new contract?

A A net $2,000 saving from avoiding staff redundancies

B Extra fixed income of $600 per month

C A reduction of $4,000 in fixed supervisors' salaries

D A $4,000 expected increase in the bad debt provision

178 Which of the following is NOT a disadvantage of using a full cost pricing system?

A It cannot account for selling and distribution costs

B The final selling price is affected by arbitrary cost allocations between products

C The mark-up used is arbitrary

D Overheads will not be fully recovered if actual volume is less than budgeted volume

179 Which of the following costs is likely to be a relevant cost for decision making (*tick all that apply*)?

	Relevant cost?
Accounting adjustments	
Incremental fixed costs	

180 Which of the following is normally considered to be a relevant cost for decision making?

A Sunk cost

B Non-incremental cost

C Committed cost

D Opportunity cost

181 Which of the following are likely to be included when setting selling prices using marginal cost pricing (*tick all that apply*)?

	Included?
Prime costs	
Direct labour supervision costs	
Variable sales distribution costs	
Depreciation on factory machinery	
Selling managers' salaries	

182 A one-off project requires 60 kg of a liquid which was purchased for $12 per kg. The liquid isn't regularly used in the business and there are 40 kg in inventory. The inventory can be sold for $4 per kg and the material would cost $15 per kg to replace.

The relevant cost of using the material in the project is $_____.

183 A manufacturer makes and sells a product with expected sales and production of 50 units per month. The accountant has also gathered the following information:

Prime cost per unit	$180
Fixed overheads per unit	$40
Non production overheads per unit	$20

This product has a dedicated investment of $500,000 and the manufacturer requires a return of 12% per annum on this investment.

To the nearest $, the price per unit to be set in order to achieve the manufacturer's target return on investment is $_____

184 Which TWO of the following statements regarding cost plus pricing are correct?

	Correct?
Marginal cost-plus pricing should be only used for short term decision making.	
Cost-plus pricing requires that the profit mark-up applied by an organisation is fixed.	
Cost-plus pricing is a strategically focused approach, as it accounts for external factors.	
Full cost-plus pricing requires the budgeted level of output to be determined at the outset.	

185 20 hours of skilled labour is required for a one-off project. Existing skilled staff are paid a fixed salary that is equivalent to $35 per hour. These staff are fully employed. Alternatively, the work could be outsourced to an agency who can provide equivalent skilled staff at $45 per hour.

The relevant cost for skilled labour in the project is $_______.

186 A business is considering closing one of its branches which has the following budgeted performance for the next year:

	$000
Revenue	200
Variable costs	(200)
Fixed costs	(150)
Budgeted profit (loss)	(150)

Variable costs include $50,000 for labour costs. These staff would have to be made redundant at a total cost of $20,000.

Fixed costs contain a fixed rent charge that is specific to the branch of $60,000 as well as $40,000 of centrally allocated costs. All other fixed costs will be saved if the branch is closed down.

What will be the net benefit for the year of shutting the branch?

A $0

B $90,000

C $150,000

D $170,000

187 A manufacturer produces three products in the same process which has joint process costs of $10,000. Details on the products are as follows:

Product	*Volume*	*Sales value per unit at the split off point*
X	400	$80
Y	200	$100
Z	400	$120

Joint process costs are allocated on the basis of sales value at the split off point. Product Z could be further processed for $2,000. This would increase the selling price per unit to $140.

To the nearest $, the net benefit from further processing Product Z is $_______.

BREAK EVEN ANALYSIS

188 A company has budgeted breakeven sales revenue of $800,000 and fixed costs of $320,000 for the next period.

What is the sales revenue needed to achieve a profit of $50,000 in the period?

A $850,000

B $925,000

C $1,120,000

D $1,200,000

189 FPG Company sells three products – F, P and G. The ratio of their total sales values is 6F : 5P : 4G. The contribution to sales ratios of the products are:

F 35% P 20% G 30%

If fixed costs for the period are expected to be $160,000, the revenue (to the nearest $1,000) needed to earn a marginal costing profit of $40,000 is:

A $598,000

B $651,000

C $698,000

D $706,000

190 R Company provides a single service to its customers. An analysis of its budget for the year ending 31 December 20X5 shows that in period 3, when the budgeted activity was 6,570 service units with a sales value of $72 each, the margin of safety was 21.015%.

The budgeted contribution to sales ratio of the service is 35%.

Budgeted fixed costs in period 3 were nearest to:

A $115,000

B $131,000

C $145,000

D $157,000

191 **Which of the following are required to determine the breakeven sales value in a multi-product manufacturing environment?**

	Required?
The product-specific fixed costs	
The product mix ratio	
General fixed costs	
The method of apportionment of general fixed costs	
Individual product gross contribution to sales ratios	

192 R Company currently sells products S, T and U in equal quantities and at the same selling price per unit. The contribution to sales ratio for product S is 60%; for product T it is 45% and the total is 52%. If fixed costs are unaffected by mix and are currently 25% of sales, the effect of changing the product mix to:

S 45% T 20% U 35%

is that the total contribution/total sales ratio changes to:

A 53.85%

B 52.00%

C 45.00%

D 33.33%

193 EFG Company manufactures three products, which have the following cost and demand data:

	Product E	*Product F*	*Product G*
Contribution to sales ratio	30%	20%	25%
Maximum sales value ($000)	1,200	1,400	1,900
Minimum sales value ($000)	400	400	400

There are fixed costs of $850,000 per period.

The lowest breakeven sales value per period, subject to meeting the minimum sales value constraints, is nearest to:

A $2,730,000

B $2,840,000

C $3,240,000

D $3,400,000

194 R Company manufactures and sells two products – S and T. Annual sales are expected to be in the ratio of 3S : 5T. Total annual sales are planned to be $640,000. Product S has a contribution to sales ratio of 32% whereas that of product T s 48%. Annual fixed costs are estimated to be $200,000.

The margin of safety is _______% *(round to one decimal place)*

195 **A company provides three different levels of customer service support for one of its software products.**

The following data relate to these three levels of support:

Support level	*Superior*	*Standard*	*Basic*
	$ per contract	*$ per contract*	*$ per contract*
Annual fee	1,000	750	400
Annual variable costs	450	250	180
Annual fixed costs (see note below)	200	100	50
Profit	350	400	170

Note*:* The total annual fixed costs are budgeted to be $1,000,000. None of these costs are specific to any type of customer service support.

Assume that the number of customer service support contracts sold are in the proportion:

Superior 20% Standard 30% Basic 50%

The annual revenue that needs to be generated in order to break even is closest to:

A $1,690,000

B $1,695,000

C $1,710,000

D $2,270,000

196 R and K Company manufactures a product that has a selling price of $14 and variable costs of $6 per unit, and incurs annual fixed costs of $24,400. Annual sales demand is 8,000 units.

A new production method is currently under consideration that would increase fixed costs by 30%, but would reduce variable costs to $5 per unit. The superior quality of the finished product would enable sales to be increased to 8,500 units per annum at a price of $15 each.

If the change in production method were to take place, what would be the breakeven output level?

A 500 units higher

B 372 units higher

C 915 units higher

D 122 units higher

197 XYZ Company sells three products.

Product X has a contribution to sales ratio of 40%.

Product Y has a contribution to sales ratio of 30%.

Product Z has a contribution to sales ratio of 35%.

Monthly fixed costs are $200,000.

The products are sold in the ratio:

X:3 Y:7 Z:5

The monthly breakeven sales revenue is $_______ (round to the nearest to $000)

198 A company has only a limited available supply of direct labour and direct materials. It manufactures two products, X and Y, for which there is unlimited sales demand at current selling prices. The resource requirements for each product are as follows:

	Product X	*Product Y*
Direct materials	2 kg	4 kg
Direct labour	3 hours	1 hour

The company seeks to maximise its profits. Each unit of product X earns a contribution of $12 per unit.

The minimum contribution that must be earned by a unit of product Y to make it worth producing units of product Y in a profit-maximising budget is $_______

199 The budgeted profit statement for Product X for next year shows that it has a margin of safety equal to 20% of budgeted sales and a unit selling price of $10. Product X has a contribution to sales (c/s) ratio of 60% and budgeted fixed costs of $120,000 for the year.

The percentage increase in the unit variable cost that would result in Product X breaking even at the budgeted level of activity is _______%

200 A business has total costs of $50,000, 70% of which are variable. Its total revenue from its single product is $40,000.

To the nearest $000, its break even sales revenue is $_______.

201 S plc produces and sells three products, X, Y and Z. It has contracts to supply products X and Y, which will utilise all of the specific materials that are available to make these two products during the next period. The revenue these contracts will generate and the contribution to sales (C/S) ratios of products X and Y are as follows:

	Product X	*Product Y*
Revenue	$10 million	$20 million
C/S ratio	15%	10%

Product Z has a C/S ratio of 25%.

The total fixed costs of S plc are $5.5 million during the next period and management has budgeted to earn a profit of $2 million.

The revenue that needs to be generated by Product Z for S plc to achieve the budgeted profit is $_______ million

202 A business makes a single product with the following standard cost card:

	$
Direct materials	8
Direct labour	14
Variable production overheads	6
Fixed production overheads	4
Total production cost	32

The budgeted production and sales for the product is 3,000 units. Selling and distribution costs total $4,000, 40% of these costs are fixed and the remainder are variable.

The product sells for $80.

To the nearest unit, the number of units to be sold in order to break-even is _______ units.

203 **If the budgeted fixed costs increase, the gradient of the line plotted on the budgeted Profit/Volume (P/V) chart will:**

A increase

B decrease

C not change

D become curvi-linear

204

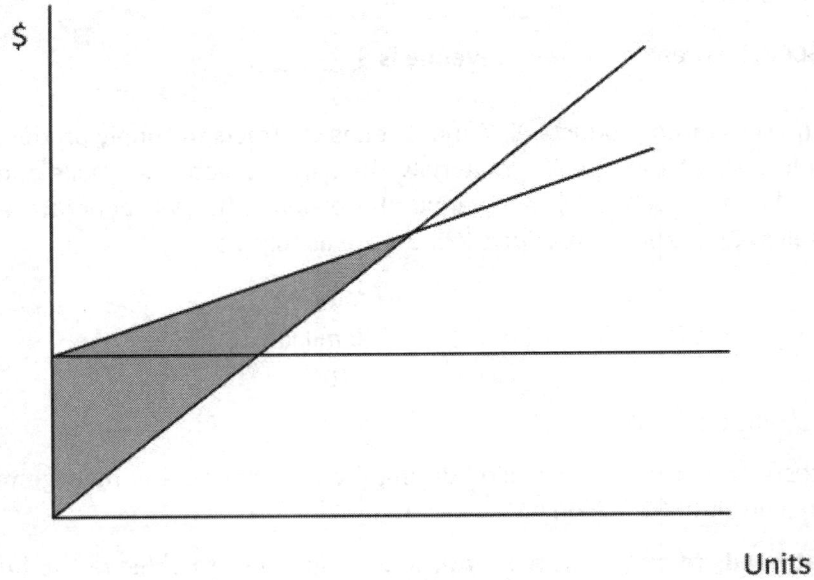

What does the shaded area on the breakeven chart above represent?

A Loss

B Fixed cost

C Variable cost

D Profit

205 A business produces a single product. Each unit has a contribution of $20. Total fixed costs are $400,000. The positive margin of safety for the product is 40% of break-even sales units.

To the nearest $000, the budgeted profit for the product is $_______.

206 A service company provides two services with the following details

Service	*Standard*	*Advanced*
	$	$
Revenue per service	40	45
Variable costs per service	10	18
Contribution per service	30	27
Budgeted number of services	50,000	20,000

The fixed costs attached to the services are $2m.

To the nearest $000, the break even sales revenue for the company is $_______.

207 An organisation sells a number of products and has created the following profit volume charts:

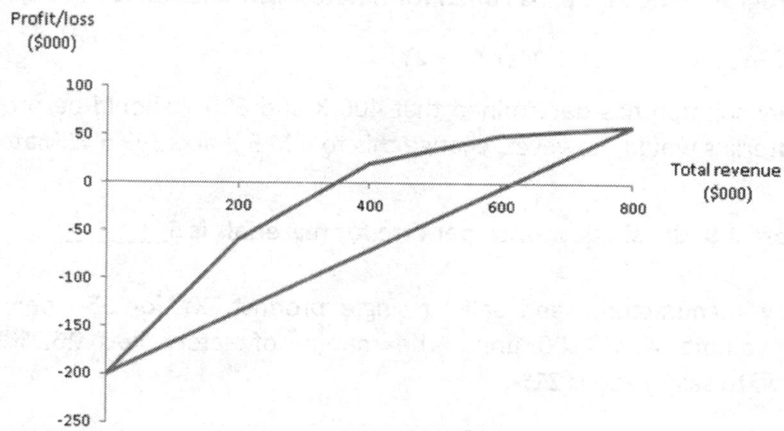

If the products are sold in the order of the most favourable contribution to sales ratio, which of the following levels of sales revenue would be closest to the organisation's break-even point?

A $200,000

B $400,000

C $600,000

D $800,000

208 Which of the following is not normally an assumption when determining the break-even point in a multi-product environment?

A The sales mix for the products remains constant

B Products are sold in order of their contribution sales ratio

C Contribution per unit for each product doesn't change

D Semi-variable costs can be split into their variable and fixed components

209 A safety training school provides two courses with details as follows:

Product	*Compulsory*	*Optional*
Percentage of budgeted sales	70%	30%
Contribution to sales ratio	75%	80%

Combined fixed costs are $22,000.

To the nearest $000, the total break even sales revenue for the products is $_______.

LINEAR PROGRAMMING

210 A linear programming model has been formulated with the following objective function:

Objective function Max 4X + 2Y

The optimal solution has determined that 400 X and 600 Y should be produced. An extra litre of materials would, however, change this to 400.5 X and 599.5 Y. Materials cost $9 per litre.

To the nearest $, the shadow price per litre for materials is $_______.

211 A company manufactures and sells a single product, XY for $56 per unit. In March, budgeted volume was 7200 units, the margin of safety was 26.2%. The budgeted contribution to sales ratio is 21%.

What are the budgeted fixed costs for March?

A $106,856

B $62,493

C $84,672

D $105,638

212 Which of the following statements is NOT true?

A Linear programming techniques should not be used when there is only one scarce resource

B Linear programming assumes that products must be made in full units

C Linear programming aims to maximise contribution to profits

D Linear programming techniques can cope with more than two scarce resources at the same time

213 An organisation is preparing a linear programming model. The company makes two products, X and Y. It needs to produce twice as many Y than X.

In the linear programming model, X will be used to represent the number of units of Product X produced and Y will be used to represent the number of units of Product Y produced.

Which of the following represents the correct constraint for the production of the products?

A $2X \geq Y$

B $X \geq 2Y$

C $X = 2Y$

D $2X = Y$

214 A company manufactures two products with the following details:

	Ultra	*Maxi*
	$	$
Selling price	60	85
Materials (@ $4 per kg)	16	12
Labour (@ $20 per hour)	20	40
Contribution	24	33

Material is a scarce resource and has a shadow price of $2 per kg. A new supplier has offered to supply extra materials but at a premium price.

The highest acceptable price per kg for the extra materials is $_______.

215 An organisation has the following contribution function:

Contribution = 12A + 8B

where

A = the number of units of product A produced, and

B = the number of units of product B produced.

A graph has identified that the optimal production plan exists at the point where the following two constraints cross:

Material X: A + 2B ≤ 8,000

Material Y: 2A + B ≤ 13,000

There is a maximum demand of 10,000 units of each product.

How many units of Product A are produced in order to maximise contribution?

A 0

B 1,000

C 6,000

D 10,000

216 An organisation is preparing a linear programming model. Its production process needs two types of labour, skilled and unskilled. There are only 4,000 hours of each available.

Usage per unit of the two types of labour for the organisation's two products is as follows:

	Skilled labour	*Unskilled labour*
Product A	5 hours	5 hours
Product B	1 hour	1 hour

In the linear programming model, X will be used to represent the number of units of Product A produced and Y will be used to represent the number of units of Product B produced.

Which of the following represents the correct constraint for unskilled labour?

A $5X + 1Y \leq 4,000$

B $5X + 5Y \leq 4,000$

C $1X + 5Y \leq 4,000$

D $1X + 1Y \leq 4,000$

217 The shadow price of skilled labour for CBV Limited is currently $8 per hour. What does this mean?

A The cost of obtaining additional skilled labour resources is $8 per hour

B There is a hidden cost of $8 for each hour of skilled labour actively worked

C Contribution will be increased by $8 per hour for each extra hour of skilled labour that can be obtained

D Total costs will be reduced by $8 for each additional hour of skilled labour that can be obtained

218 E Limited manufactures four products from different quantities of the same material which is in short supply. The following budgeted data relates to the products:

	Product E1	*Product E2*	*Product E3*	*Product E4*
	$/unit	$/unit	$/unit	$/unit
Selling price	90	112	123	103
Materials ($6 per kg)	24	33	41	30
Conversion costs	40	65	65	55
	64	98	106	85
Profit	26	14	17	18
Machine time per unit in hours	0.5	0.5	0.6	0.6

The conversion costs include general fixed costs that have been absorbed using a rate of $30 per machine hour.

The ranking for the most profitable use of the raw materials is to make product:

	1st	*2nd*	*3rd*	*4th*
A	E1	E4	E2	E3
B	E1	E4	E3	E2
C	E3	E2	E4	E1
D	E4	E2	E1	E3

219 Q plc makes two products – Quone and Qutwo – from the same raw material. The selling price and cost details of these products are as shown below:

	Quone	*Qutwo*
	$	$
Selling price	20.00	18.00
Direct material ($2.00 per kg)	6.00	5.00
Direct labour	4.00	3.00
Variable overhead	2.00	1.50
Contribution per unit	8.00	8.50

The maximum demand for these products is:

Quone	500 units per week
Qutwo	unlimited number of units per week

If material were limited to 2,000 kgs per week, the shadow price of these materials would be:

A $nil

B $2.00 per kg

C $2.66 per kg

D $3.40 per kg

220 The following details relate to three services provided by RST Company:

	Service R	*Service S*	*Service T*
	$	$	$
Fee charged to customers	100	150	160
Unit service costs:			
Direct materials	15	30	25
Direct labour	20	35	30
Variable overhead	15	20	22
Fixed overhead	25	50	50

All three services use the same type of direct labour which is paid $25 per hour.

The fixed overheads are general fixed overheads that have been absorbed on the basis of machine hours.

If direct labour is a scarce resource, the most and least profitable uses of it are:

	Most profitable	*Least profitable*
A	S	R
B	S	T
C	T	R
D	T	S

221 The following equations have been taken from the plans of DX for the year ending 31 December 20X5:

Contribution (in dollars) = 12 X1 + 5 X2 + 8 X3

Materials: 2 X1 + 3 X2 + 4 X3 = 12,000 kilos

Machine hours: 6 X1 + 4 X2 + 3 X3 = 8,000 machine hours

$0 \leq X1 \leq 2{,}000$

$100 \leq X2 \leq 500$

$0 \leq X3 \leq 200$

where: X1, X2, and X3 are the number of units of products produced and sold,

If an unlimited supply of raw material could be obtained at the current price, the product mix that maximises the value of DX plc's contribution is:

	X1	*X2*	*X3*
A	1,333	0	0
B	1,233	0	200
C	1,166	100	200
D	1,241	100	50

222 BJS Company uses three components, P, Q and R, in its main product. The budget for next year indicates a requirement for 3,000 of each component. The components are all manufactured on the same machine, for which only 50,000 hours are available next year. The variable cost of internal manufacture of each component together with the machine hours used are shown in the table below. The table also shows prices quoted by a sub-contractor for supplying the components.

Component	*Machine hours per unit*	*Variable cost $ per unit*	*Sub-contractor $ per unit*
P	9	45	65
Q	5	70	78
R	12	56	80

The minimum total cost (to the nearest $000) at which BJS Company can obtain the full requirement of components is $_______

223 An organisation has created the following linear programming solution to represent the position it faces currently in the presence of short term scarce resources:

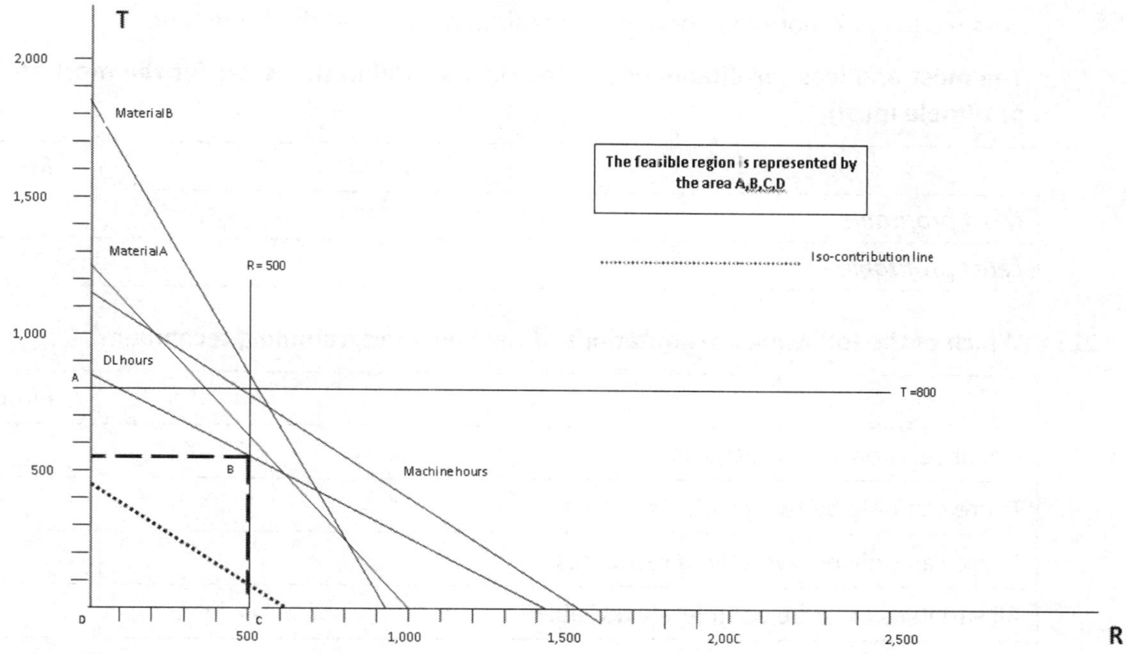

Note: DL = Direct labour hours

The point marked B has been determined to be the point which provides the optimal production plan.

Which of the following resources will have a shadow price greater than 0? (tick all that apply)

	Shadow price >0?
Direct labour hours	
Material A	
Material B	
Machine hours	

224 The following details relate to ready meals that are prepared by a food processing company:

Ready meal	*K* *$/meal*	*L* *$/meal*	*M* *$/meal*
Selling price	5.00	3.00	4.40
Ingredients	2.00	1.00	1.30
Variable conversion costs	1.60	0.80	1.85
Fixed conversion costs*	0.50	0.30	0.60
Profit	0.90	0.90	0.65
Oven time (minutes per ready meal)	10	4	8

*The fixed conversion costs are general fixed costs that are not specific to any type of ready meal.

Each of the meals is prepared using a series of processes, one of which involves cooking the ingredients in a large oven. The availability of cooking time in the oven is limited and, because each of the meals requires cooking at a different oven temperature, it is not possible to cook more than one of the meals in the oven at the same time.

The most and least profitable use of the oven is: (fill in the letter for the most and least profitable meal)

	Meal?
Most profitable	
Least profitable	

225 Which of the following are limitations of the linear programming technique?

	Limitation?
Linear relationships must exist	
There can only be two products	
There can only be two scarce resources	
All variables must be completely divisible	
A computer must be used to find the optimal point	

226 JRL manufactures two products from different combinations of the same resources. Unit selling prices and unit cost details for each product are as follows:

Product	*J*	*L*
	$/unit	*$/unit*
Selling price	115	120
Direct material A ($10 per kg)	20	10
Direct material B ($6 per kg)	12	24
Skilled labour ($14 per hour)	28	21
Variable overhead ($4 per machine hour)	14	18
Fixed overhead	28	36

Which of the following equations represents the iso-contribution line?

A 13J + 11L = M

B 41J + 47L = M

C 54J + 58L = M

D 54J + 65L = M

227 An organization has created the following linear programming solution to represent the position it faces currently in the presence of short term scarce resources:

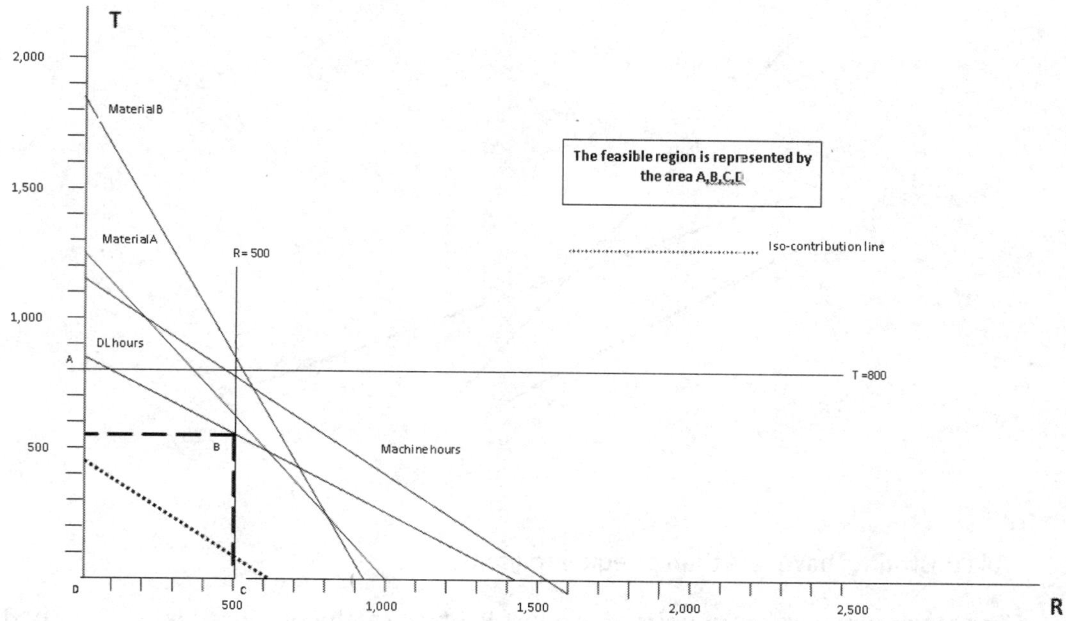

The organisation manufactures two products, T and R. Each T requires 1.4 kgs of material A and each R requires 2 kgs of material A.

The maximum amount of Material A available is _______ kgs

228 An organisation has the following contribution function:

Contribution = 12A + 8B, where

A = the number of units of product A produced, and

B = the number of units of product B produced.

A graph has identified that the optimal production plan exists at the point where the following two constraints cross:

Material X: A + 2B ≤ 8,000

Material Y: 2A + B ≤ 13,000

There is a maximum demand of 10,000 units of each product.

How many units of Product A are produced in order to maximise contribution?

A 0

B 1,000

C 6,000

D 10,000

229 An organisation has graphed the following linear programming model:

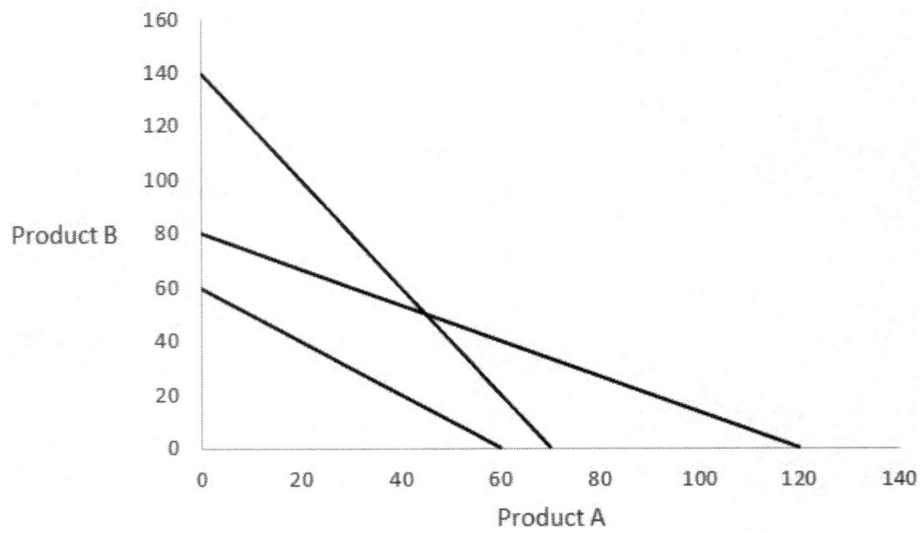

All constraints have less than or equal to limits.

The maximum number of units of Product B which can be produced is _______ units.

230 An organisation has the following contribution function:

Contribution = 5X + 10Y

where

X = the number of units of product X produced, and

Y = the number of units of product Y produced.

A graph has identified that the optimal production plan exists at the point where the following two constraints cross:

Skilled labour: $6X + 4Y \leq 62{,}000$

Unskilled labour: $2X + 5Y \leq 50{,}000$

There is a maximum demand of 12,000 units of each product.

The number of units of Product Y produced in order to maximise contribution (to the nearest whole unit) is _______ units.

DEALING WITH UNCERTAINTY IN THE SHORT TERM

231 The daily demand for a perishable product has the following probability distribution:

Demand (units)	*Probability*
100	0.25
200	0.40
300	0.35

Each item costs $4 and is sold for $8. Unsold items are thrown away at the end of the day.

If orders must be placed before the daily demand is known, the number of units that should be purchased at the beginning of each day in order to maximise expected profit is _______ units

232 A company has estimated the selling prices and variable costs of one of its products as follows:

Selling price per unit		*Variable cost per unit*	
$	Probability	$	Probability
40	0.30	20	0.55
50	0.45	30	0.25
60	0.25	40	0.20

The company will be able to supply 1,000 units of its product each week irrespective of the selling price. Selling price and variable cost per unit are independent of each other.

The probability that the weekly contribution will exceed $20,000 is _______% *(round to the nearest whole %)*

233 X Company can choose from five mutually exclusive projects. The projects will each last for one year only and their net cash inflows will be determined by the prevailing market conditions. The forecast annual cash inflows and their associated probabilities are shown below:

Market conditions	*Poor*	*Good*	*Excellent*
Probability	0.20	0.50	0.30
	$000	$000	$000
Project L	500	470	550
Project M	400	550	570
Project N	450	400	475
Project O	360	400	420
Project P	600	500	425

Based on the expected value of the net cash inflows, which project should be undertaken?

A L

B M

C N

D P

234 A baker is trying to decide the number of batches of a particular type of bread that he should bake each day. Daily demand ranges from 10 batches to 12 batches. Each batch of bread that is baked and sold yields a positive contribution of $50, but each batch of bread baked that is not sold yields a negative contribution of $20.

Assuming the baker adopts the *minimax regret* decision rule, the number of batches of bread that he should bake each day is _______ batches

235 **Match the decision criterion with the assumed approach to risk taken by the decision maker *(draw a line connecting the decision criteria to the correct attitude to risk)***

Decision criteria
Expected values
Maximax
Maximin
Minimax regret

Attitude to risk
Risk averse
Risk averse
Riske neutral
Risk seeker

236 A company is making a decision on whether to launch a new product. The decision is illustrated in the following decision tree:

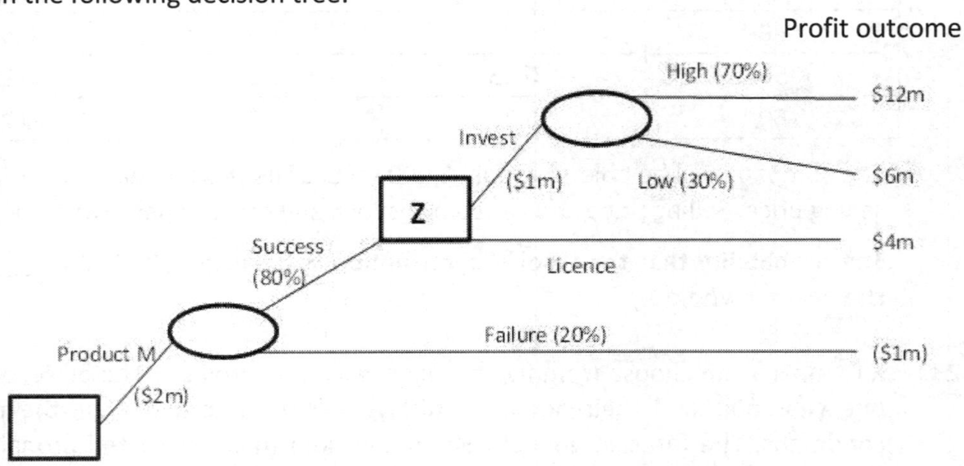

The profit outcomes do not include the cost of any investments made.

The expected value at point Z is $9.2m.

What is the overall expected value from the product launch?

A $5.16m

B $7.16m

C $7.36m

D $9.20m

237 On investigating the labour efficiency variance an organisation has found that there is typically a favourable variance of mean of $60,000 and a standard deviation of $5,000.

The probability that the variance is less than $45,000 is _____% *(answer to two decimal places)*

238 Chris orders bunches of flowers from a wholesaler which he then sells on his market stall. Chris has to order the flowers before the demand is known, any unsold flowers are thrown away at the end of the day.

A payoff table below shows the profits Chris can expect based upon the quantity he orders and the level of demand.

	Order level			
Demand	20 bunches	30 bunches	40 bunches	50 bunches
20 bunches	$60	$20	$(20)	$(60)
30 bunches	$60	$90	$50	$10
40 bunches	$60	$90	$120	$80
50 bunches	$60	$90	$120	$150

Using a minimax regret table, the order level that would be selected if Chris applied the minimax regret decision criterion is:

A 20 bunches

B 30 bunches

C 40 bunches

D 50 bunches

239 Yum, a chocolate manufacturer, has to decide which of three new chocolate bars to launch. Demand is uncertain and could occur at one of three levels: low, medium or high. The management accountant uses expected values to make this type of decision and this has resulted in predicted expected profit of $142,000.

The market is highly competitive and so Yum has decided to employ the services of a market research company who can provide perfect information about the likely demand level.

Yum is prepared to pay a maximum of $15,000 for the information from the market research company.

To determine the value of this information Yum had to calculate the expected profit with the information, what was the value of that expected profit?

A $157,000

B $127,000

C $112,000

D $97,000

240 **Perfect information is described as:**

A 100% accurate

B 85% accurate

C Sometimes accurate

D Never accurate

241 P Company currently sells 90,000 units of product Y per annum. At this level of sales and output, the selling price and variable cost per unit are $50 and $21 respectively. The annual fixed costs are $1,200,000. The management team is considering lowering the selling price per unit to $45.

The estimated levels of demand at the new price, and the probabilities of them occurring, are:

Selling price of $45

Demand	*Probability*
100,000 units	0.45
120,000 units	0.55

It is thought that at either of the higher sales and production levels, the variable cost per unit, and the probability of it occurring, will be as follows:

Variable cost (per unit)	*Probability*
$20	0.40
$18	0.60

The probability that lowering the selling price to $45 per unit would increase profit is _______% *(round to the nearest whole %)*

242 A company expects to sell 1,000 units per month of a new product but there is uncertainty as to both the unit selling price and the unit variable cost of the product. The following estimates of selling price, variable costs and their related probabilities have been made:

Selling price		*Unit variable cost*	
$ per unit	Probability	$ per unit	Probability
20	25%	8	20%
25	40%	10	50%
30	35%	12	30%

There are specific fixed costs of $5,000 per month expected for the new product.

What is the expected value of monthly contribution?

A $5,890

B $10,300

C $10,890

D $15,300

243 **Which of the following are disadvantages of using an expected value technique?**

	Disadvantage of EVs?
Expected values only provides the most likely result	
It ignores attitudes to risk	
Only two possible outcomes can be considered	
Probabilities are subjective	
The answer provided may not exist	

244 The committee of a new golf club is setting the annual membership fee. The number of members depends on the membership fee charged and economic conditions. The forecast annual cash inflows from membership fees are shown below.

Membership fee	*Membership level*		
	Low	*Average*	*High*
	$000	$000	$000
$600	360	480	540
$800	400	440	480
$900	360	405	495
$1,000	320	380	420

What would be the fee set by the committee if the maximin criterion is applied?

A $600

B $800

C $900

D $1,000

245 Sarah owns a cafe and is trying to decide how many cakes she should bake each day. The demand is uncertain and Sarah has to make the cakes at the start of each day before the demand level is known.

The payoff table below shows the daily contribution Sarah can expect depending on the number of cakes baked and the level of demand that occurs.

	Number of cakes baked		
Level of demand	20	25	30
Low	$14	$11.5	$9
Medium	$14	$17.5	$15
High	$14	$17.5	$21

The number of cakes Sarah should bake if she applies the maximax decision criterion is ______

246 X Company can choose from five mutually exclusive projects. The projects will each last for one year only and their net cash inflows will be determined by the prevailing market conditions. The forecast annual cash inflows and their associated probabilities are shown below:

Market conditions	*Poor*	*Good*	*Excellent*
Probability	0.20	0.50	0.30
	$000	$000	$000
Project L	500	470	550
Project M	400	550	570
Project N	450	400	475
Project O	360	400	420
Project P	600	500	425

What would be the value of perfect information about the state of the market?

A Nil

B $5,000

C $26,000

D $40,000

247 A company is trying to decide which of four products it should launch. The demand is uncertain and is based on optimistic, likely and pessimistic forecasts. A regret matrix has been prepared showing the regret for each of the outcomes depending on the decision made.

Regret matrix	*Product*			
Demand forecast	*W*	*X*	*Y*	*Z*
Optimistic	$43,000	$0	$73,000	$38,000
Likely	$15,000	$5,000	$35,000	$0
Pessimistic	$0	$17,000	$42,000	$25,000

If the company applies the minimax regret criterion to make decisions, which product would be chosen?

A W

B X

C Y

D Z

248 A company is considering launching one of two new products. If the product is successful in its first month there will be an opportunity to either make a further investment or to licence all future development to another company. The decision for the company is illustrated by the following decision tree:

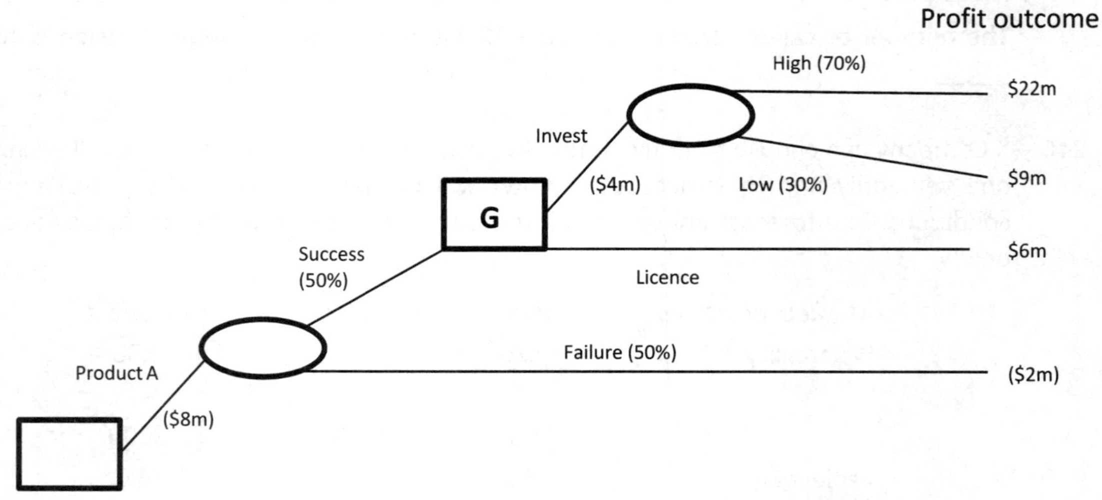

The profit outcomes do not include the cost of any investments made.

What is the expected value at point G?

A $6m

B $14.1m

C $18.1m

D $20.1m

249 A toy retailer is considering introducing a new product and has to decide if the sales price should be $100, $105, $110 or $115. There is a 30% chance that demand could be high, a 50% chance that demand will be at a medium level and a 20% chance that demand will be low.

A payoff table below shows the profits based upon the sales price and the level of demand.

	Sales price			
Demand	$100	$105	$110	$115
High	$1,700,000	$1,725,000	$1,700,000	$1,625,000
Medium	$700,000	$600,000	$450,000	$250,000
Low	$100,000	$60,000	$0	$(80,000)

The retailer has decided, using an expected value approach, the sales price should be set at $100 as this gives the highest expected profit of $880,000.

A market research company has since approach the retailer, it believes it can provide perfect information on the demand level.

The maximum amount that should be paid for the information from the market research company is $_______ *(Answer should be given to the nearest whole $)*

250 Soggy makes paddling pools and has to decide in advance how many pools to make before the summer demand is known. Demand is determined by the weather, if it is very hot and sunny demand will be high, if it is a rainy cold summer demand will be low and a warm summer will result in average demand.

The budgeted profit for the current year is $1,190,000. The profit for the previous year was very low due to a wet summer so Soggy is considering employing the services of a meteorologist to predict the likely weather for this summer. The predictions are not perfect but should give a good indication.

Soggy has decided that it is prepared to pay a maximum of $30,000 for the meteorologist services as using the predictions should result in an expected profit of $1,250,000.

What is the expected profit for Soggy Ltd if the meteorologist had not been employed?

A $1,280,000

B $1,250,000

C $1,220,000

D $1,190,000

251 A national chain of coffee shops has three potential new sites available:

		SHOP SIZE		
Demand	*Probability*	*Small*	*Medium*	*Large*
Strong	0.2	354,600	894,300	1,413,200
Good	0.4	172,100	529,300	865,700
Weak	0.4	80,850	255,550	226,950

If the management team used an expected value approach they would have decided to open a large shop as this give the highest expected value of $719,700.

A market research company believes it can provide perfect information on the potential demand level.

The maximum amount that should be paid for the information from the market research company is $_______ *(Answer should be given to the nearest whole $)*

252 Sarah owns a cafe and is trying to decide how many cakes she should bake each day. The demand is uncertain and Sarah has to make the cakes at the start of each day before the demand level is known.

The payoff table below shows the daily contribution Sarah can expect depending on the number of cakes baked and the level of demand that occurs.

	Number of cakes baked		
Level of demand	20	25	30
Low	$14	$11.5	$9
Medium	$14	$17.5	$15
High	$14	$17.5	$21

The number of cakes Sarah should bake if she applies the maximin decision criterion is _____

253 The committee of a new golf club is setting the annual membership fee. The number of members depends on the membership fee charged and economic conditions. The forecast annual cash inflows from membership fees are shown below.

	Membership level		
Membership fee	*Low*	*Average*	*High*
	$000	$000	$000
$600	360	480	540
$800	400	440	480
$900	360	405	495
$1,000	320	380	420

What would be the fee set by the committee if the minimax regret criterion is applied?

A $600

B $800

C $900

D $1,000

254 P Company currently sells 90,000 units of product Y per annum. At this level of sales and output, the selling price and variable cost per unit are $50 and $21 respectively. The annual fixed costs are $1,200,000. The management team is considering lowering the selling price per unit to $45.

The estimated levels of demand at the new price, and the probabilities of them occurring, are:

Selling price of $45

Demand	*Probability*
100,000 units	0.45
120,000 units	0.55

It is thought that at either of the higher sales and production levels, the variable cost per unit, and the probability of it occurring, will be as follows:

Variable cost (per unit)	*Probability*
$20	0.40
$18	0.60

The expected value of the company profit if the selling price is reduced to $45 per unit is $_______

255 A company is considering launching one of two new products. If the product is successful in its first month there will be an opportunity to either make a further investment or to outsource all future development to another company. The decision for the company is illustrated by the following decision tree:

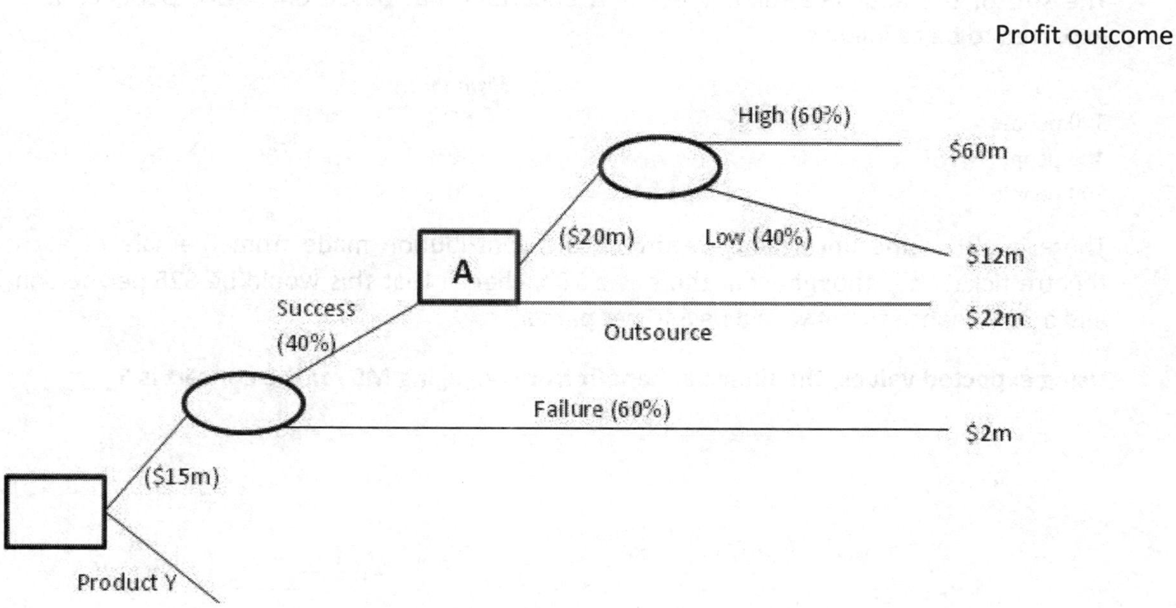

The profit outcomes do not include the cost of any investments made.

The expected value at point A on the decision trees (to the nearest $0.1m) is $_____m

256 A company expects to sell 1,000 units per month of a new product but there is uncertainty as to both the unit selling price and the unit variable cost of the product. The following estimates of selling price, variable costs and their related probabilities have been made:

Selling price		*Unit variable cost*	
$ per unit	Probability	$ per unit	Probability
20	25%	8	20%
25	40%	10	50%
30	35%	12	30%

There are specific fixed costs of $5,000 per month expected for the new product.

What is the probability of monthly contribution from this new product exceeding $13,500?

A 24.5%

B 30.5%

C 63.0%

D 92.5%

257 A theatre has a seating capacity of 500 people and is considering engaging MS and her orchestra for a concert for one night only. The fee that would be charged by MS would be $10,000. If the theatre engages MS, then this sum is payable regardless of the size of the theatre audience.

The size of the audience for this event is uncertain, but based on past experience it is expected to be as follows:

	Probability
300 people	50%
400 people	30%
500 people	20%

There is also some uncertainty regarding the contribution made from the sale of each theatre ticket. It is thought that there is a 70% chance that this would be $25 per person and a 30% chance that it would be $40 per person.

Using expected values, the financial benefit from engaging MS for the concert is $_____

Section 2

ANSWERS TO OBJECTIVE TEST QUESTIONS

COST ACCOUNTING FOR DECISION AND CONTROL

RATIONALE FOR COSTING

1 B

Reporting is the main purpose of financial accounting. The main purposes of management accounting are planning, control and decision making.

2

	Management accounting	Financial accounting
Uses only historical data		✓
Is carried out at the discretion of management	✓	
Uses non-financial information	✓	
Aids planning within the organisation	✓	

3

	Strategic?
Making day-to-day decisions about the running of a department	
Defining the objectives of the company	✓
Deciding in which markets to operate	✓
Deciding about how to compete within their chosen markets	
Inventory control	

Strategic level management would normally define the objectives of the company and make decisions about which markets to operate in. Tactical level managers would then decide how best to operate in these markets while operational level managers would make day-to-day decisions required in running their departments such as inventory control.

4 B

Direct costs are those costs which can be economically identified with a single cost unit.

5 D

Although total fixed costs are the same at all levels of activity, the fixed cost per unit falls as the activity level increases. The unit cost does not fall in a straight line, but in a curve as shown in the question.

6 B

Managers are not usually classified as direct labour, because their salary cost cannot be traced to specific cost units.

TRADITIONAL COSTING

7 B

	$
Marginal costing profit	45,000
Less: fixed cost included in opening inventory (28,000 – 16,000)	(12,000)
Plus: fixed cost included in closing inventory (36,400 – 20,800)	15,600
Absorption costing profit	48,600

Alternative approach

Increase in inventory using marginal costing	$4,800
Increase in inventory using absorption costing	$8,400
Difference = fixed overhead absorbed in inventory	$3,600

Inventory is increasing so absorption costing profit is higher than marginal costing profit by the amount of fixed overhead absorbed.

Absorption costing profit = $45,000 + $3,600 = $48,600

8 B

The opening inventory was 400 units and the closing inventory was 900 units, therefore inventory has increased.

If production is greater than sales then absorption costing will show the higher profit.

Difference in profit: = Change in inventory × Fixed production cost per unit
= (900 – 400) × $29,500/5,000 units = $2,950

9 A

OAR = $330,000/220,000 = $1.50 per unit

	$
Overhead absorbed (200,000 units × $1.50)	300,000
Actual overhead	260,000
Over absorbed	40,000

10 The profit for the period using absorption costing is $7,170

Value of closing inventory =$(13,500 + 11,800 + 32,400) × 200/2,000 = $5,770

	$	$
Sales (1,800 × $45)		81,000
Cost of production	57,700	
Less closing inventory	5,770	
Cost of sales		51,930
Gross profit		29,070
Non-production overhead		21,900
Profit		7,170

11 D

		Correct?
(i)	A cost driver is any factor that causes a change in the cost of an activity.	✓
(ii)	For long-term variable overhead costs, the cost driver will be the volume of activity.	✓
(iii)	Traditional absorption costing tends to under-allocate overhead costs to low-volume products.	✓

Statement (i) provides a definition of a cost driver. Cost drivers for long-term variable overhead costs will be the volume of a particular activity to which the cost driver relates, so Statement (ii) is correct. Statement (iii) is also correct. In traditional absorption costing, standard high-volume products receive a higher amount of overhead costs than with ABC. ABC allows for the unusually high costs of support activities for low-volume products (such as relatively higher set-up costs, order processing costs and so on).

12 The profit for the period using marginal costing is $3,930.

Value of closing inventory = $(13,500 + 11,800) × 200/2,000 = $2,530

	$	$
Sales		81,000
Variable cost of production	25,300	
Less closing inventory	2,530	
Cost of sales		22,770
Contribution		58,230
Fixed overhead		54,300
Profit		3,930

13 A

	$
Actual overhead incurred	481,250
Less under-absorbed overhead	19,250
Overhead absorbed	462,000

Overhead absorbed = Actual standard hours charged × OAR

So OAR = overhead absorbed/actual standard hours charged = $462,000/38,500 = $12

OAR = Budgeted overheads/budgeted labour hours

So budgeted overheads = OAR × budgeted labour hours = $12 × 38,000 = $456,000

14 B

OAR = $500,000/2,000 = $250 per unit

Inventory has fallen by 300 units in the period.

Absorption costing profit will be 300 × $250 = $75,000 lower than marginal costing profit as some fixed overhead from previous periods will be brought forward to be matched against sales in the period using absorption costing. In marginal costing only the fixed overhead incurred in the period will be included in the profit statement.

15 C

Option A may lead to over-absorption but this will depend on the extent to which actual overhead costs differ from budget. Option B describes under-absorption. Option D refers to budgeted overheads, which are used to calculate the OAR but otherwise not used in the calculation of under-/over-absorption.

16 The under-/over-absorption of fixed production overheads for the assembly department is $480.

	Assembly	*Finishing*	*Stores*	*Maintenance*	*Total*
Budgeted overhead	100,000	150,000	50,000	40,000	340,000
Reapportion maintenance	16,000	18,000	6,000	(40,000)	–
			56,000		
Reapportion stores	33,600	22,400	(56,000)		–
Total overhead	149,600	190,400			340,000

OAR for assembly department = $149,600/100,000 = $1.496 per unit

	$
Overhead absorbed 120,000 × 1.496	179,520
Overhead incurred	180,000
Under-absorption	480

17 A

	$000	$000
Sales revenue		820
Variable cost of sales		
Variable production costs	300	
Less: closing inventory	45	255
Variable selling costs		105
Contribution		460
Fixed costs		
Production	180	
Selling	110	290
Profit		170

Working

The closing inventory is valued at cost. As it is a marginal costing system the inventory is valued at variable cost, i.e. $300,000/1,000 units = $300 per unit. The closing inventory is 150 units, therefore the closing inventory value is $300/unit × 150 units = $45,000.

18 The total gross profit for the deluxe speedboat using absorption costing is $16,800.

Fixed production overheads = $69,600,000

Budgeted machine hours = (1,000 × 100) + (1,200 × 200) + (800 × 300) = 580,000

Fixed production overhead absorption rate = $69,600,000/580,000 = $120 per machine hour

	Deluxe
	$000
Sales	86,400
Direct material	27,400
Direct labour	13,400
Production overhead	28,800
Gross profit	16,800

ACTIVITY BASED COSTING

19

		Facility-sustaining	*Product-sustaining*
(i)	General staff administration	✓	
(ii)	Plant management	✓	
(iii)	Technical support for individual products and services		✓
(iv)	Updating of product specification database		✓
(v)	Property management	✓	

20 A

$$\text{Cost driver rate} = \frac{\text{Budgeted cost of orders}}{\text{Budgeted number of orders}} = \frac{\$110,010}{2,895} = \$38 \text{ for each order}$$

	$
Cost recovered: 210 orders × $38	7,980
Actual costs incurred	7,650
Over-recovery of costs for four-week period	330

21 The cost per unit attributed to product r for machine set ups is $0.52

Machine set up costs for Product R

Budgeted machine set-ups:

Product D (1,000 × 3)	=	3,000
Product R (2,000 × 4)	=	8,000
Product P (2,000 × 6)	=	12,000
		23,000

$$\text{Cost per set up} = \frac{\$150,000}{23,000} = \$6.52$$

$$\text{Budgeted unit cost of R:} = \frac{\$6.52 \times 4}{50} = \mathbf{\$0.52}$$

22 The total cost attributed to product Y for component deliveries using the proposed activity based costing system is $2,160

Cost driver	*Number of cost drivers*	*Charge out rate*
Number of component deliveries	500 + 600 + 800 = 1,900	$6,840/1,900 = $3.60 per delivery

Charge to Product Y = 600 × $3.6 = $2,160

23 The cost per unit attributed to product L for processing time is $0.16

Budgeted processing minutes:

Product L (300,000 × 4)	=	1,200,000	
Product M (300,000 × 6)	=	1,800,000	
Product N (150,000 × 6)	=	900,000	
		3,900,000	minutes

Cost per minute = $\frac{\$156,000}{3,900,000}$ = $0.04

Budgeted unit cost of L = $0.04 × 4 = **$0.16**

24 The total cost attributed to product c for quality inspections using an activity based costing system is $8,484

Cost driver	*Number of cost drivers*	*Charge out rate*
Number of quality inspections	(200 × 10) + (300 × 20) + (400 × 30) = 20,000	$14,140/20,000 = $0.707 per inspection

Charge to Product C = 400 × 30 × $0.707 = $8,484

25 Advantages of an activity based costing system

Cost	*Advantage?*
Better cost control is possible	✓
Arbitrary allocations of costs are avoided	
Better product pricing is possible	✓
The choice of cost drivers is easy	
Can be applied to service companies	✓

ABC provides better information on costs and how they are driven. It should therefore facilitate better cost control it can be difficult to attach cost drivers to activities and this can make the system expensive to set up initially. It will also still involve some arbitrary cost allocations. For example, in a service industry it may be difficult to determine what drives the chief executive's salary and to determine how this should be allocated to services.

Despite these faults, ABC should still provide a *better* allocation of costs to products when compared to traditional costing methods and this should then result in better pricing decisions. The success of ABC in manufacturing industries has led to the adoption of the technique in service industries – and exam questions are just as likely to involve service industries as they are to involve a manufacturing company.

OTHER ELEMENTS OF COSTING

26 C

Return per minute $= \dfrac{\text{Selling price} - \text{material cost}}{\text{Time on bottleneck resource}}$

$= \dfrac{50-16}{8}$

$=$ €4.25

Return per hour $=$ €4.25 × 60 = €255

27 The throughput accounting ratio for this product is 0.778.

Return per factory hour = $\dfrac{\$12 - \$5}{0.75\text{ hrs}}$ = $9.333

Cost per factory hour = $144,000/12,000 = $12

TA ratio = 9.3333/12 = 0.778

28 Process **Y** is the bottleneck process.

	Product S	*Product T*
Throughput of process X per day		
	$13.5\text{ hrs} \times \dfrac{60}{5} = 162.00$	$13.5\text{ hrs} \times \dfrac{60}{7.5} = 108.00$
(Production time: 15 – 1.5 = 13.5 hours)		
Throughput of process Y per day		
	$14\text{ hrs} \times \dfrac{60}{18} = 46.67$	$14\text{ hrs} \times \dfrac{60}{12} = 70.00$
(Production time: 15 – 1 = 14 hours)		

Process Y is the bottleneck process because it limits the production of both products to figures that are less than sales demand.

29 A

This is the CIMA *Official Terminology* definition of a bottleneck. With a throughput accounting approach, the aim should be to reduce or remove bottlenecks, so as to increase throughput.

30 The value of inventory of X at 31 August using a throughput accounting approach is $5,000.

Under throughput accounting, finished goods will be valued at direct material cost.

$$\text{Cost per unit} = \frac{\$40,000}{2,000 \text{ units}} = \$20 \text{ per unit}$$

No. of units in closing inventory = 2,000 – 1,750 = 250 units.

Therefore value of closing inventory = 250 units × $20 = $5,000

31 D

Using throughput accounting inventory is valued at material cost

Inventory value = 20,000/4,000 × 400 units = $2,000

32 The profit for the period using throughput accounting is $2,750.

Value of closing inventory = $13,500 × 200/2,000 = $1,350

	$	$
Sales		81,000
Material costs	13,500	
Less closing inventory	1,350	
Cost of sales		12,150
Throughput		68,850
Operating expenses		66,100
Net profit		2,750

33 The return per hour for product b is $780.

	A	*B*	*C*
	$	$	$
Selling price	200	150	150
Direct materials	41	20	30
Throughput	159	130	120
Machine P – minutes per unit	12	10	7
Return per factory minute	159/12 13.25	130/10 13	120/7 17.14
Return per factory hour × 60 minutes	$795	$780	$1,028

34 A

Digital products typically have a low or nil marginal cost. They do not typically have high marginal costs.

The other statements are true.

35

	Higher	**Lower**
The life span of the product	✓	
The total indirect labour costs	✓	
Inventory costs		✓
Infrastructure costs	✓	

Digital products typically have longer/higher life spans than physical products as they can be more easily updated with new features. Total indirect labour costs also tend to be higher because of this need to provide ongoing updates and support. There will also be infrastructure costs such as payments to have the product on a particular mobile platform (such costs are typically absent for physical products). But no inventory will be held of digital products and therefore these costs will not exist.

36 A

Although it may happen, it is not common for systems to be linked to those of customers. This would not impact on the costing of the product.

37 B

Digital products typically have a low or nil marginal cost. Marginal costing would not be useful for digital products.

38

	True	**False**
There is a focus on a smaller number of suppliers		✓
Fewer overhead drivers are used		✓
Large volumes of data are processed	✓	
The digital cost can be created very quickly	✓	

Digital costing provides access to a greater number of suppliers. It also provides more details on overheads and has more overhead drivers. But it can deal with large volumes of data and provide products costs almost instantaneously.

VARIANCE ANALYSIS

39 The favourable material price variance is $836.

The standard price per kg = $5

The actual price paid per kg = $82,764 / 16,720 kg = $4.95 per kg

The price variance = $0.05 per kg x 16,720 kg = $836

40 C

Option A is an ideal standard, option B is an attainable standard and option D is a current standard.

41 D

Direct labour variance

					$	
AHSR						
	24,000 hrs	×	$15/hr	=	360,000	$24,000 F Rate
AHAR				=	336,000	

42 A

Variable overhead variance

					$	
SHSR						
	2 hrs/unit × 11,000 units	×	$6/hr	=	132,000	Efficiency $12,000 A
AHSR						
	24,000 hrs	×	$6/hr	=	144,000	

43 D

	$
Budget overhead	2,500,000
Actual overhead	2,010,000
Expenditure variance	490,000 F

44 C

OAR = $2,500,000/500,000 = $5 per unit

Budgeted volume	500,000 units
Actual volume	440,000 units
	60,000 units
× OAR per unit	× $5
Volume variance	$300,000 A

45 A

	$
Expected cost = ($800 + $0.0002 × $4,100^2$) × 1.03	4,287
Actual cost	5,000
	713A

46 B

Inventories are valued at standard prices, so the material price variance must be calculated by reference to the quantity purchased.

Material variances

				$		
SQSP						
	6 kg/unit × 2,192 units	×	$6.75/kg	= 88,776	}	Usage
AQSP						
	13,050 kg	×	$6.75/kg	= 88,087.50	}	$688.50 F

For a usage variance the quantity must be the quantity used (13,050 kgs).

				$		
AQSP						
	12,550 kg	×	$6.75/kg	= 84,712.50	}	$11,812.50 F
AQAP						
				= 72,900	}	Price

For a price variance the quantity must be the quantity purchased (13,050 kgs – reduction in inventory = 13,050 – 500 = 12,550 kgs).

Alternatively:

	$	
12,550 kgs should cost ($6.75/kg)	84,712.50	
They did cost	72,900.00	
Price variance	$11,812.50	(F)

	kgs	
Usage variance		
2,192 finished units should use (× 6)	13,152	
They did use	13,050	
Usage variance in kgs	102 kgs	(F)

Usage variance in $ = 102 kgs (F) × $6.75/kg (standard price) = $688.50 (F)

47 C

Actual hours paid = 9,760

Actual hours work = 9,480

Difference = 280 hours

Standard rate = $24

Idle time variance = $6,720

48 C

Labour variances

					$	
SHSR						
	10 hrs/unit × 6,200 units	×	$9.50/hr	=	589,000	Efficiency
AHSR						$8,455 A
	62,890 hrs	×	$9.50/hr	=	597,455	
AHAR						$1,043 F
				=	596,412	Rate

The variances could also be calculated as follows:

Rate variance:	$	
62,890 hours should cost (× $9.50)	597,455	
They did cost	596,412	
Labour rate variance	1,043	(F)

Efficiency variance:	*Hours*	
6,200 units should take (× 10)	62,000	
They did take	62,890	
Efficiency variance in hours	890	(A)

Efficiency variance in $ = 890 hours (A) × $9.50 per hour = $8,455 Adverse.

49 The adverse fixed overhead volume variance is $10,000.

Absorption rate = $\frac{\$170,000}{42,500}$ = $4/unit

	Units	
Budgeted output	42,500	
Actual output	40,000	
Volume variance in units	2,500	(A)
Standard fixed overhead cost/unit	× $4	
Fixed overhead volume variance in $	$10,000	(A)

50 The favourable fixed overhead efficiency variance is $24,000.

		Hours	
Standard hours for actual production	(104,040/20,400) × 20,000	102,000	
Less Actual hours		100,000	
Volume variance in units		2,000	(F)
Standard fixed overhead cost/hour	($1,248,480/104,040)	× $12	
Fixed overhead efficiency variance in $		$24,000	(F)

51 B

Actual hours		660	
Less Budgeted hours	2 × 320 ops	640	
Capacity variance in hours		20	(F)
Standard fixed overhead cost/hour	($108,000/[320 × 2 hours])	× $168.75	
Fixed overhead capacity variance in $		$3,375	(F)

52 D

Standard hours for actual production	2 hours × 300 ops	600	
Less Actual hours		660	
Efficiency variance in hours		60	(A)
Standard fixed overhead cost/hour	($108,000/[320 × 2 hours])	× $168.75	
Fixed overhead efficiency variance in $		$10,125	(A)

53 C

Variable overhead variance

					$	
AHSR	8,000 hrs	×	$15/hr	=	120,000	$12,000 A Expenditure
AHAR				=	132,000	

The variance could also be calculated as follows:

	$	
8,000 hours should cost × $15)	120,000	
did cost	132,000	
Expenditure variance	12,000	Adverse

54 B

				$	
SHSR					
0.75 hrs/unit × 11,000 units	×	$20/hr	=	165,000	Efficiency
AHSR					$5,000 F
8,000 hrs	×	$20/hr	=	160,000	

The variances could be calculated as follows:

	Hours	
11,000 units should take (× 0.75 hr)	8,250	
did take	8,000	
Efficiency variance in hours	250	Favourable
Standard rate per hour	× $20	
Efficiency variance in $	$5,000	Favourable

55 D

Sales price variance

	$	
Std selling price	500	
Actual selling price	465	
Sales price variance	35	(A)
× Actual no of units sold	× 642	
	22,470	

56 C

Sales volume contribution variance

	Units	
Budgeted quantity sold	600	
Actual quantity sold	642	
Sales volume variance in units	42	(F)
× Std contribution per unit (25% × $500)	× $125	
	$5,250	(F)

57 A

The fixed overhead volume variance is the difference between budgeted and actual production volume multiplied by the standard absorption rate per unit. This is the same as the difference between budgeted value of fixed overheads (budgeted volume × standard absorption rate per unit) and standard fixed overheads absorbed by actual production (actual volume × standard absorption rate per unit).

58

		Correct?
(i)	The standard allowance for material wastage was set too high.	
(ii)	Material purchased was of a lower quality than standard.	✓
(iii)	Lower grade and less experienced employees were used than standard.	✓
(iv)	More material was purchased than budgeted for the period because output was higher than budgeted.	

Event (i) is more likely to result in a favourable usage variance therefore it is not correct. Event (ii) could cause an adverse usage variance since a lower quality material might lead to higher wastage and a higher level of quality control rejects. Event (iii) could cause an adverse usage variance because lower skilled employees might waste material and quality control rejects might again be higher. Event (iv) would not necessarily cause an adverse usage variance. The usage variance is based on the expected usage for the actual output, not on the budgeted usage for the budgeted output.

59 **The favourable inspection efficiency variance for December is $4,000.**

Total budgeted inspections = $30,000 / $200 = 150 inspections

Standard inspections on actual output = 150 x 1,200 units / 1,000 units = 180 inspections

Efficiency variance = (180 inspections – 160 inspections) x $200 per inspection = $4,000 favourable

60 **B**

Less experienced employees are likely to take longer than standard to produce a given level of output. The result would be an adverse variable overhead efficiency variance. Option A is more likely to result in a favourable variable overhead efficiency variance because employees are likely to work faster than standard. Option C might also result in a favourable efficiency variance because higher quality material is likely to be easier to process, thus saving time against standard. Option D would result in an adverse variable overhead expenditure variance but would not directly affect the variable overhead efficiency variance.

61 **The favourable sales volume profit variance for the period was $20,000.**

Sales volume profit variance

Budgeted sales volume (units)	100,000	
Actual sales volume (units)	110,000	
	10,000	favourable
Standard profit per unit ($10 – $8)	$2	
	$20,000	Favourable

62 D

The question is telling us two things: firstly, that actual hours were greater than budgeted hours, and, secondly, that actual hours were more than the standard hours. The first point would lead to a favourable fixed overhead capacity variance. The second point would result in an adverse labour efficiency and fixed overhead efficiency variances. If the standard hours are 100 more than the original budget then it would result in a favourable fixed overhead volume variance.

63 The idle time variance for April was $49,500.

Idle hours = 61,500 – 56,000 = 5,500

Standard rate per hour = $540,000/60,000 = $9

Idle time variance = 5,500 × $9 = $49,500 Adverse

64

Variance
Material price variance
Material usage variance
Labour rate variance
Labour efficiency variance

Cause
Increase in costs charged by a supplier
Increased wastage due to a machine malfunction
Unexpected pay award
Improved operating procedures for staff

An increase in costs from a supplier would cause an adverse material price variance. Increased wastage would cause an adverse material usage variance but might not affect labour efficiency. An unexpected pay award would give an adverse labour rate variance, and improved operating procedures would make the staff more efficient and as such a favourable efficiency variance.

65

	Caused by purchasing better quality?
Favourable fixed overhead expenditure variance	
Favourable material usage variance	✓
Adverse labour rate variance	
Favourable labour efficiency variance	✓
Favourable labour rate variance	

66 B

It is usual for the purchasing department to negotiate prices with suppliers. So if a supplier is charging more than the standard price this would fall under the responsibility of the purchasing manager.

Better quality materials should result in less wastage of material which in turn will allow the employees to produce more units in the time allowed as fewer units will be scrapped or require rework.

67 A

It is usual for the production manager to finalise the production schedule so if the labour has been less efficient than expected then this would be his responsibility.

68

	Affected?
Sales price variance	
Sales quantity profit variance	✓
Fixed overhead expenditure variance	
Fixed overhead capacity variance	✓

The difference in between marginal and absorption costing is in the treatment of fixed overheads. This will impact on the profit per unit which will impact on the sales quantity profit variance. In marginal costing there is no fixed overhead volume variance and therefore there would be no fixed overhead capacity variance.

69 The expenditure variance for the set ups was $100.

Standard price (SP) = 6,820/220 = 31

Flexed standard cost = AQ × SP = 200 × $31 = 6,200

Actual cost = 6,300

Variance = 6,200 – 6,300 = $100A

70 The favourable variable overhead efficiency variance is $3,000

Number of hours per unit for Product X = $14/$7 = 2 hours

Number of hours per unit for Product Y = $10.50/$7 = 1.5 hours

Variable overhead cost per hour = $3/2 hours (or $2.25/1.5 hours) = $1.50 per hour

Variable overhead efficiency variance =

((12,000 × 2 hrs) + (16,000 × 1.5 hrs)) – 46,000) × $1.50 per hour = $3,000 Favourable

71 B

Standard quantity (SQ) = 75 supervisors/5,000 employees × 5,500 employees = 82.5 supervisors

Standard price (SP) = $7,500/75 supervisors = $100 per supervisor

Standard cost (SQ × SP) = 82.5 × $100 = $8,250

Actual cost = $8,085

Total variance = 8,250 – 8,085 = $165 Favourable

72 The favourable sales price variance is $17,400

The actual selling price = $365,400 / 58 audits = $6,300.

The sales price variance = ($6,300 - $6,000) x 58 audits = $17,400

73 B

When using a marginal costing system the sales volume variance will be based on the standard contribution per unit.

The volume variance is 5,000 units, and the total value = 5,000 x 20 = $100,000

74 The total adverse materials variance was $32,200

Expected materials cost per poster = 6 × $10 = $60

Total expected cost for the actual campaign = $60 × 20,000 posters = $1,200,000

Actual cost = $1,232,200

Total variance = 1,200,000 - 1,232,200 = $32,200 adverse

75 The favourable variable overhead efficiency variance is $3,000

The standard rate per hour = $60

The actual rate per hour = $120,900/1,950 hours = $62

The rate variance = $2 × 1,950 hours = $3,900

Alternatively:

The standard cost of actual hours = $60 × 1,950 = $117,000

The actual cost = $120,900

The variance = $117,000 – $120,900 = $3,900 adverse.

76 D

The standard cost for the 500 actual units produced = 240,000 × $10 = $2.4m

The actual cost = $2.51m

Total variance = $2.4m – $2.51m = $110,000 adverse

FURTHER VARIANCE ANALYSIS

77 The actual rate paid per direct labour hour for the period was $12.75

11,500 units should use 5 hours each	57,500 hours
Did use	?
Variance in hours	
Value at $12 per hour	
Labour efficiency variance	$30,000 A

Working backwards:

The variance in hours = $30,000/12 = 2,500 A

The actual hours used are 57,500 + 2,500 = 60,000

60,000 hours should cost (× $12)	720,000
Did cost	?
Labour rate variance	45,000 A

Working backwards:

The actual labour cost = $765,000

So the actual rate paid per hour = $765,000/60,000 = $12.75.

78 The total favourable sales mix profit variance for the period using the individual units method is $50.

Product	Standard mix	Actual mix	Variance (units)	Standard profit/unit	Sales mix variance
A	725	750	25 (F)	$5.00	$125.00 (F)
B	725	700	25 (A)	$3.00	$75.00 (A)
Total	1,450	1,450			$50.00 (F)

Where the standard mix is the total actual sales units (1,450) divided by the total budgeted sales units (1,600) and multiplied by the budgeted units of each individual product (800 for A)

79 The favourable sales mix profit variance for Product B is $26,250.

	Actual sales @standard mix (units)	Actual sales @ actual mix (units)	Variance (units)	Standard profit $	Variance $
Product B	2,475	3,000	525 F	50.00	26,250 F
Product C	2,025	1,500	525 A	53.75	28,219 A
	4,500	4,500			1,969 A

80 The total favourable sales quantity profit variance for the period using the individual units method is $5,130.

Standard weighted average profit per unit

Product	Sales budget (units)	Standard profit/unit	Total profit
A	3,000	$2.00	$6,000
B	8,000	$1.50	$12,000
C	9,000	$1.80	$16,200
Total	20,000		$34,200

Average profit per unit = $34,200/20,000 units = $1.71 per unit

Sales quantity profit variance

Budgeted sales units	20,000	
Actual sales units	23,000	
	3,000	(F)
Average profit per unit	$1.71	
Sales quantity profit variance	$5,130	(F)

81 C

Total budgeted profit = ($4 × 4,000) + ($3 × 6,000) = $34,000

Weighted average profit per unit = $34,000/10,000 = $3.40

	Actual sales @standard mix (units)	*Budget sales @ standard mix* (units)	*Variance* (units)	*Standard profit* $	*Variance* $
Product R	4,800	4,000	800 F	3.40	2,720 F
Product S	7,200	6,000	1,200 F	3.40	4,080 F
	12,000	10,000			6,800 F

82 The adverse material price planning variance was $4,480.

Material price planning variance

Original standard price	$4.10
Revised standard price	$4.50

.40 A × 11,200 units = $4,480 A

83 C

				$	
SQSP					
6 kg/unit × 600 units	×	$3/kg	=	10,800	
AQSP					Usage $450 F
	×	$3/kg	=		
AQAP					$2,000 F
	×		=		Price

This is a 'backwards' question. Given some information including the variances, we then have to work backwards to find some missing numbers – here, the number of kg purchased.

				$	
SQSP					
6 kg/unit × 600 units	×	$3/kg	=	10,800	Usage
AQSP					$450 F
3,450 kg[Bal 2]	×	$3/kg	=	10,350[Bal 1]	
AQAP					$2,000 F
	×		=		Price

The question can also be answered as follows:

	Kg	
600 units should use (× 6 kg)	3,600	
Usage variance in kg ($450(F)/3)	150	(F)
Therefore 600 units did use	3,450	

Given no change in stock levels, usage quantity = purchase quantity.

84 B

Material variance

					$	
SQSP	3 kg/unit × 10,000 units	×	$5/kg	=	150,000	Usage $10,000 A
AQSP	32,000 kg	×	$5/kg	=	160,000	
AQAP	32,000 kg	×	$4.80/kg	=	153,600	$6,400 F Price

The standards here are the revised standards.

85 B

	Planning		Operational	
Original		Revised Standard		Actual Standard
$4		$5		$4.80

Planning price variance = ($4 – $5) × 3 kg × 10,000 units = $30,000 A

86 The total adverse sales mix profit variance for the period using the individual units method is $600.

Standard weighted average profit per unit

Product	*Sales budget (units)*	*Standard profit/unit*	*Total profit*
A	800	$5.00	$4,000
B	800	$3.00	$2,400
Total	1,600		$6,400

Sales quantity profit variance

Budgeted sales units	1,600	
Actual sales units	1,450	
	150	(A)
Average profit per unit	$4	
Sales quantity profit variance	$600	(A)

Average profit per unit = $6,400/1,600 units = $4.00 per unit

87 D

				$	
SQSP	3 kg/unit × 10,000 units	×	$5/kg	= 150,000	Usage $10,000 A
AQSP	32,000 kg	×	$5/kg	= 160,000	
AQAP	32,000 kg	×	$4.80/kg	= 153,600	$6,400 F Price

The standards here are the revised standards.

88 The adverse operational material usage variance was $3,600.

Operational material usage variance

1,600 units should use (× 7)	11,200 kg
did use	12,000 kg
	800 kg A

Valued at revised standard price ($4.50) $3,600 A

89 The favourable sales mix variance for concessions for the exhibition is $12,000

	Full price	Concessions
Actual sales (visitors)	12,000	8,000
Actual sales in standard mix	15,000	5,000
Variance (visitors)		3,000 F
Standard contribution		$4
Variance ($)		12,000 F

90 The total favourable sales mix profit variance for the period using the individual units method is $620.

Product	*Standard mix*	*Actual mix*	*Variance (units)*	*Standard profit/unit*	*Sales mix variance*
A	3,450	4,000	550 (F)	$2.00	$1,100 (F)
B	9,200	7,500	1,700 (A)	$1.50	$2,550 (A)
C	10,350	11,500	1,150 (F)	$1.80	$2,070 (F)
Total	23,000	23,000			$620 (F)

91 A

	$	
SHSR		
$\frac{12}{60}$ × 370 × $10/hr =	740	Efficiency $60 A
AHSR		
80 hrs × $10/hr =	800	

92 The actual level of production for the period was 360,000 units

OAR = $1,500,000/300,000 = $5 per unit

Fixed production overhead variance is the level of over/under absorption. An adverse variance means that overhead is under absorbed.

	$
Overhead absorbed	
Actual output × $5	?
Actual overhead	1,950,000
Under absorbed	150,000

93 The actual quantity of materials purchased in May was 8,630 kg

Actual cost – material price variance = the standard price for actual materials

$56,000 - $4,220 = $51,780

Actual materials quantity = $51,780/ $6 = 8,630 kg

BUDGETING AND BUDGETARY CONTROL

PREPARING BUDGETS

94

	Purpose of budgeting?
Communication	✓
Authorisation	✓
Sales maximisation	
Co-ordination	✓

The budget communicates to individual managers what is expected of them in the forthcoming budget period and how much expenditure they can incur in meeting their targets. Thus communication is a purpose of budgeting. An agreed budget provides authorisation for individual managers to incur expenditure in undertaking the activities in their own budget centre. Therefore authorisation is a purpose of budgeting. Although an organisation might have an objective of maximising sales and might set a budget to enable them to achieve this objective, the maximisation of sales is not in itself a purpose of budgeting. Therefore is not correct. Individual budget targets are set within the framework of the plan for the organisation as a whole and in this way a budget provides a means of coordinating the efforts of everyone within the organisation.

95 C

The cash budget is part of the master budget.

The other statements are all true.

96 D

Sales units:

	1	2	3
Sales units	2,500	3,000	4,000

Opening inventory = 10% of quarter 2 sales = 10% × 3,000 = 300

Closing inventory = 10% of quarter 3 sales = 10% × 4,000 = 400

Production = sales + closing inventory – opening inventory

= 3,000 + 400 – 300 = 3,100 units

97 C

Note that the material usage figure is not required.

	Units
Sales	30,000
Add closing inventory (3,500 × 1.35)	4,725
Less opening inventory	(3,500)
Production	31,225

98 A

The increasing use of electronic devices makes big cata collection easier. Many organisations successfully gather information from social media sites such as Facebook and Twitter and use it to great effect within their decision-making processes.

99

	E	*F*	*G*	*Total*
Budgeted number of batches to be produced:	75,000/200 = 375	120,000/60 = 2,000	60,000/30 = 2,000	
Machine set-ups per batch:	5	3	9	
Total machine set-ups	1,875	6,000	18,000	25,875

So budgeted cost per set-up: $180,000/25,875 = $6.96 per set-up

Therefore the budgeted machine set-up cost per unit of F produced is:

($6.96 × 3)/60 = $0.35 per unit or $6.96 × 6,000/120,000 = $0.35 per unit

100 D

101 The expected level of production in May is 15,900 units

	April	*May*	*June*
Production budget (units)			
Sales	12,000	15,000	18,000
Add closing inventory	4,500	5,400	
	16,500	20,400	
Less opening inventory	3,600	4,500	
Production	12,900	15,900	

102 A

Beyond budgeting makes greater use of rolling budgets to create an environment of continuous planning. It also has more local budget setting (rather than a top-down approach), uses a greater number of targets (rather than simply focusing on financial targets) and seeks continuous improvements (rather than standardisation).

103 B

A zero based budgeting system begins each budget from scratch every time. All expenditure on the activity must be justified from zero and the method of carrying out each activity must be re-evaluated as if it were being carried out for the first time.

104 C

Probability of rainy summer = $1.0 - 0.4 = 0.6$

Expected value of sales volume = $(80,000 \times 0.4) + (120,000 \times 0.6)$

= 104,000 units

105

	True	False
Big Data management involves using sophisticated systems to gather, store and analyse large volumes of data	✓	
Data can be in variety of structured and unstructured formats.	✓	
Big data does not include traditional data from internal sources such as sales history, preferences, order frequency and pricing information.		✓
Big Data does include information from external sources such as websites, trade publications and social networks.	✓	

106 The value for purchases of J to be included in the cash budget for February is $36,400

	January units	*February units*
Materials budget		
Production (units)	4,300	5,300
× No. of units of material per unit of product	× 1 unit	× 1 unit
Usage quantity (units)	4,300	5,300
Add closing inventory	1,325	
	5,625	
Less op inventory	1,075	
Purchase quantity (units)	4,550	
× purchase price	× $8	
Purchase cost ($)	36,400	

The purchase cost of materials in January is $36,400. This will be paid in February.

107 The budgeted cost per month for quality testing is $34,000

$$\text{The monthly variance} = \frac{\$102{,}000}{12 \text{ months}} = \$8{,}500$$

$$\text{The variance number of tests} = \frac{\$8{,}500}{\$850 \text{ per test}} = 10 \text{ tests}$$

Budgeted tests must therefore have been = 50 – 10 = 40 per month.

Budgeted quality test costs per month = 40 tests × $850 per test = $34,000

108 D

This is the definition of a master budget.

109 The entry for 'purchases' that will be shown in the cash budget for August is $76,000

September are $86,000

October are $106,000

Purchases are sold at cost plus 25% so cost of sales is 100/125= 0.8 × Sales

Closing inventory = 0.5 × Following month's cost of sales

Closing inventory = Opening inventory of the following month

Month	*Sales*	*Cost of sales*	*Opening inventory*	*Closing inventory*	*Purchase*	*Paid*
July	100	80	40	36	76	
August	90	72	36	50	86	**76**

110 The total receipts expected in month 4 are $114,144

	Sales	$
Cash receipts	$108,000 × 20%	21,600
Month 2	$120,000 × 80% × 40% × 0.985	37,824
Month 1	$105,000 × 80% × 58%	48,720
B/f		6,000
		$114,144

111 The budgeted profit per unit for Product X using activity-based budgeting is $48.40

Overhead cost per unit	*X*
	$
Receiving/inspecting quality assurance (W1)	504,000
Production scheduling/machine set-up (W2)	390,000
Total overhead cost	894,000
Units produced and sold	15,000
Overhead cost per unit	59.60

Activity based profit from Product X	$
Selling price	183.00
Direct material	40.00
Direct labour	35.00
Overhead cost per unit	59.60
Profit per unit	48.40

Workings

(W1) 1,800/5,000 × 1,400,000 = 504,000

(W2) 260/800 × 1,200,000 = 390,000

112 The material purchases budget for the next year is $656,400

Budgeted sales	24,000	units
Plus closing inventory	2,000	units
Less opening inventory	(500)	units
Budgeted production	25,500	units

Raw material required	25,500 units × 2 kg	= 51,000 kg
Plus closing inventory	2,000 units × 2 kg	= 4,000 kg
Less opening inventory		(300) kg
Raw material purchases		54,700 kg
Raw material purchases budget	54,700 kg × $12	= $656,400

113 The labour cost budget for the year is $2,112,000

Labour hours for production

36,000 units × 4 hours = 144,000 hours

Idle time = 10% of total available hours, therefore total available hours need to be:

144,000 hours/0.9 = 160,000 hours

Labour cost budget ($)

160,000 hours × 20% = 32,000 hours × ($12 × 1.50) = $576,000

160,000 hours × 80% = 128,000 hours × $12 = $1,536,000

The total labour cost budget = 576,000 + 1,536,000 = $2,112,000

114 The budgeted trade payable days at the end of next year are 41 days

Trade payables outstanding at end of this year = $474,500/365 × 45 = $58,500

Purchases budget for next year = $474,500 × 1.1 = $521,950

Trade payable days at end of next year = $58,500/$521,950 × 365 = 40.9 days

115 C

	$
Cash received from previous period	460,000
Sales for this budget period	5,400,000
	5,860,000
Credit sales not paid until next period ($5,400,000 × 80% × 1/12)	(360,000)
Total cash received	5,500,000

116 The material purchases budget for the forthcoming year is $556,000

Production budget for Product D

	Units	
Opening inventory	(6,000)	
Sales	36,000	
Closing inventory	3,000	i.e. 36,000/12
Production	33,000	

Purchases budget for raw material C

	kg	
Opening inventory	(2,000)	
Production	66,000	i.e. 33,000 × 2 kg
Closing inventory	5,500	i.e. (33,000/12) × 2 kg
Purchases	69,500	

The purchases budget for raw material C is therefore:

69,500 kg × $8 per kg = $556,000

117 The answer is $4,933,500

Budgeted sales	144,000	units
Plus Closing inventory	12,000	units
Less Opening inventory	(6,500)	units
Budgeted production	149,500	units

149,500 × 2 hours per unit = 299,000 hours

80% × 299,000 = 239,200 hours × $15 = $3,588,000

20% × 299,000 = 59,800 hours × $(15 × 1.5) = 1,345,500

Total labour cost budget = $4,933,500

118 B

119

Cost
Commission paid to an agent for selling the product
Electricity used in the factory
Depreciation of factory building
Packaging material to protect the product

Budget
Selling overhead budget
Variable production overhead budget
Fixed production overhead budget
Distribution overhead budget

120 The entry for 'purchases' that will be shown in the cash budget for September is $86,000

Purchases are sold at cost plus 25% so cost of sales is 100/125= 0.8 × Sales

Opening inventory = 0.5 × this month's cost of sales

Closing inventory = 0.5 × following month's cost of sales

Closing inventory = Opening inventory of the following month

Month	*Sales*	*Cost of sales*	*Opening inventory*	*Closing inventory*	*Purchase*	*Paid*
August	90	72	36	50	86	
September	125	100	50	56	106	**86**

121 C

	$
Cash paid from previous period	540,000
Purchases for this budget period	6,800,000
	7,340,000
Purchases not paid until next period ($6,800,000 × 75% × 1/12)	(425,000)
Total cash paid	6,915,000

122 A

The annual rent for the head office building is an administrative overhead not a production overhead, the electricity usage would be a variable production overhead rather than a fixed production overhead, and the materials is a direct cost rather than an overhead.

123 C

The direct material and the royalty fee are both direct costs and therefore not included with in the overhead budget.

124 The budgeted fixed overheads in the period were $200,000

As the overheads are absorbed on a labour hours basis the number of units and machine hours are irrelevant. So the budget will be 16,000 hours × $12.50 per hour = $200,000

125 C

Total labour hours = (1,000 units × 0.5 hours) + (2,000 units × 2 hours) = 4,500 hours

Total machine hours = (1,000 units × 0.25 hours) + 2,000 units × 1.5 hours) = 3,250 hours

Total variable overheads = 3,250 hours × $1.50 per hour = $4,875

Total fixed overheads = 4,500 hours × $1.95 per hour = $8,775

Total overheads = $4,875 + $8,775 = $13,650

126

	Not a criticism?
It may make managers, staff and unions feel threatened	✓
It encourages slack	
It is time consuming as it involves starting from scratch	✓
It encourages wasteful spending	
It includes past inefficiencies as costs are not scrutinised	

ZBB may make staff feel threatened as they need to justify all costs and activities. This is less likely with incremental budgeting. Incremental budgeting is not a slow process, as budgets are based on prior period figures.

127

	Characteristic of rolling budgets?
Budgets are more likely to be realistic as there is a shorter period between preparation and actual events occurring	
Updates to budgets are only made when they are foreseeable	✓
They reduce uncertainty in budgeting	
They force management to look ahead more frequently	
Each item of expenditure must be fully justified before inclusion in the budget	✓

Rolling budgets are updated on as regular basis (for example, monthly or quarterly), not just when a change is foreseeable. The final point is a characteristic of zero based budgeting.

128 D

Zero based budgeting is the method in which all activities are re-evaluated.

129 D

130 D

Month	*1*	*2*	*3*
Production units	1,850	1,800	2,020
Rate per unit	$1.20	$1.20	$1.20
Variable overhead cost	$2,220	$2,160	$2,424
60% in month	1,332	1,296	1,454
40% in following month		888	864
Payment	1,332	2,184	2,318

131 The sales receipts for month 2 are budgeted to be $10,180

Month	*1*	*2*	*3*
Sales units	1,500	1,750	2,000
Sales (Units × $10)	15,000	17,500	20,000
Paid in month – 20% × 0.98	2,940	3,430	3,920
45% in the following month		6,750	7,875
25% in 3rd month			3,750
Receipts	2,940	10,180	15,545

132 A

Zero based budgeting starts each year from scratch.

FORECASTING

133 D

Production overhead:

	Units		$
High	800	(× 1.75)	1,400
Low	500	(× 2.50)	1,250
	300		150

Variable cost = $150/300 = $0.50. Fixed cost = $1,400 – (800 × $0.50) = $1,000

Other overhead:

	Units		$
High	800	(× 0.625)	500
Low	500	(× 1.00)	500

This is a wholly fixed cost.

Period fixed cost:	$	Variable cost per unit	$
Fixed production overhead	1,000	Direct material	2.00
Other overhead	500	Direct labour	1.50
		Variable production overhead	0.50
	1,500		4.00

134 D

Year 2, quarter 3 is period 7

Trend sales = 22,000 + 800 (7)
= 27,600 units

Adjusted for seasonal variations = 27,600 + 7,080 = 34,680 units

135 C

High Low Method	*Activity*	$	
	6,500	33,000	
	4,500	29,000	
Difference	2,000	4,000	
So the variable cost	= $4,000/2,000	= $2 per unit	
Substitute into either activity	6,500	33,000	Total cost
	6,500 × $2	13,000	Variable cost
	Difference	$20,000	Fixed cost

The estimated production cost for 5,750 units = 5,750 × $2 + $20,000 = $31,500

136 C

At output of 6,000 units, overhead = 6,000 × $3.20 = $19,200

At output of 10,000 units, overhead = 10,000 × $3.00 = $30,000

Therefore variable overhead/unit = $\frac{\$30{,}000 - \$19{,}200}{10{,}000 - 6{,}000}$ = $2.70

Fixed overhead = $19,200 – (6,000 × $2.70) = $3,000

At activity of 7,350 units, budgeted production overhead = $3,000 + (7,350 × $2.70) = $22,845

137 B

Variable cost per unit = ($2,840,000 – $2,420,000)/(190,000 – 160,000)
= $420,000/30,000
= $14 per unit

Fixed costs = $2,840,000 – (190,000 × $14)
= $180,000

Total costs at 205,000 units = (205,000 × $14) + $180,000
= $3,050,000

138 The overhead cost for RP for month 240 is $39,000

Orders = [100,000 + (30 × 240)] × 1.08 = 115,776

Overhead cost = $10,000 + ($0.25 × 115,776) = $38,944

139 D

Trend	=	9.72 + (5.816 × 23)
	=	143.488
Seasonal factor	+	6.5
Forecast		149.988

To the nearest whole unit, the forecast number of units to be sold is 150.

140 The total fixed costs for a budgeted output of 36,000 units are $86,000

It is known that there is a stepped fixed cost of $10,000 above 35,000 units. Removing the stepped fixed cost at 40,000 units leaves $184,000.

(i) Variable cost per unit = $\dfrac{\$184{,}000 - \$143{,}500}{40{,}000 - 25{,}000}$ = $2.70

(ii) At 25,000 units

Total cost	143,500
Total variable cost $2.70 × 25,000	67,500
Fixed cost	76,000

Therefore fixed cost at 36,000 units = $76,000 + $10,000 = $86.000

141 C

	Machine hours	$
High	12,212	39,477
Low	8,480	31,080
Change	3,732	8,397

Variable cost per machine hour	=	$8,397/3,732
	=	$2.25
Fixed cost = $39,477 – (12,212 × $2.25)	=	$12,000

Budget cost allowance for 9,340 machine hours:

		$
Fixed cost		12,000
Variable cost (9,340 × $2.25)	=	21,015
		33,015

142 After adjusting for seasonal variations, the expected sales of Product A for Quarter 3 of Year 2 is 30,000 units

Quarter	*Trend sales units*	*Actual sales units*	*Variation units*
1	13,000	14,000	+1,000
2	16,000	18,000	+2,000
3	19,000	18,000	–1,000
4	22,000	20,000	–2,000

Year 2 Quarter 1 = 10,000 + (3,000 × 5) = 25,000 + 1,000 = 26,000 units

Year 2 Quarter 2 = 10,000 + (3,000 × 6) = 28,000 + 2,000 = 30,000 units

Year 2 Quarter 3 = 10,000 + (3,000 × 7) = 31,000 – 1,000 = 30,000 units

143 B

Variable cost per unit

$$\frac{\text{Change in cost}}{\text{Change in units}} \quad \frac{113{,}000 - 55{,}000}{3{,}000 - 1{,}000} = \$29.00/\text{Unit}$$

Total fixed cost

Total cost @ 3,000 units	113,000
Less variable cost (3,000 units × $29.00/unit)	87,000
Total fixed cost	$26,000

Flexed budget for 2,750 units

Variable cost (2,750 units × $29.00/unit)	79,750
Fixed cost	26,000
Total cost	$105,750

144 C

Cost before stepped increase = $2,840,000 – $30,000 = $2,810,000

Variable cost per unit = ($2,810,000 – $2,420,000)/(190,000 – 160,000)

= $390,000/30,000 = $13

Fixed costs at 190,000 units = $2,840,000 – (190,000 × $13)

= $370,000

Total costs at 175,000 units = (175,000 × $13) + ($370,000 – $30,000)

= $2,615,000

145

89% of the variation in production costs from one month to the next can be explained by corresponding variation in output.	✓
Costs increase as output increases.	
The linear relationship between output and costs is very strong.	✓
An increase of 100% in output is associated with an increase of 89% in costs.	
An increase of 89% in output is associated with an increase of 100% in costs.	

A coefficient of determination between output and production costs, tells us that 89% of the variation in production costs from one month to the next can be explained by corresponding variation in output. It also tells us that the linear relationship between output and costs is very strong. Only a positive correlation can tell us that costs increase as output increases and we cannot assume this from the coefficient of determination.

146 C

By use of the high/low method

Variable cost per unit

$$\frac{\text{Change in cost}}{\text{Change in units}} \quad \frac{24{,}000 - 18{,}000}{2{,}000 - 1{,}000} = \$6/\text{Unit}$$

Total fixed cost

Total cost @ 2,000 units	24,000
Less variable cost (2,000 units × $6/unit)	12,000
Total fixed cost	$12,000

Flexed budget for 1,980 units

Variable cost (1,980 units × $6/unit)	11,880
Fixed cost	12,000
Total cost	$23,880

BUDGETARY CONTROL

147

	Limitations of 'What if' analysis?
Only one variable changes at a time	✓
It assesses the risk to the closing cash balance	
It provides an assessment of how responsive the cash flows are to changes in variables.	
Probabilities of changes are not accounted for	✓
It directs attention to critical variables	

The other options are advantages of using what if analysis.

148 C

Revised fixed costs = $1,600k - $400k + $250k + $900k (20% x cost of sales) = $2,350k

Contribution = ($6,800k - $3,600) x 60% = $1,920k

Revised profit / (loss) = $1,920k - $2,350k = ($430k)

Fall in profit = $700 + $430k = $1,130k

149 C

Budgetary slack is also called budget bias. Budget holders may sometimes try to obtain a budget that is easier to achieve. They may do this either by bidding for expenditure in excess of what they actually need or, in the case of sales budgets, by deliberately setting easy revenue targets.

150 The total adverse profit variance for the period was $5,040

	Original budget	*Flexed budget*	*Actual*	*Variances*
Sales units	1,000	1,380	1,380	
Sales revenue	100,000	138,000	133,860	4,140 (A)
Direct material	40,000	55,200	57,800	2,600 (A)
Direct labour	20,000	27,600	27,000	600 (F)
Variable overhead	15,000	20,700	18,600	2,100 (F)
Fixed overhead	10,000	10,000	11,000	1,000 (A)
Profit	15,000	24,500	19,460	5,040 (A)

151 D

A is a fixed budget. B is a zero based budget. C is a flexed budget

152 A

This is an example of feed-forward control, as the manager is using a forecast to assist in making a future decision.

153 B

	Original Budget	*Flexed Budget*
Sales units	1,000	1,200
	$	$
Sales revenue	100,000	120,000
Direct material	40,000	48,000
Direct labour	20,000	24,000
Variable overhead	15,000	18,000
Fixed overhead	10,000	10,000
Profit	15,000	20,000

154 A

155 B

156 C

157 C

The net cash flow in month 4 will fall by $300k. This will increase the closing cash balance to $410,000. This is $160k above the overdraft limit of $250k.

This would represent ethical (rather than unethical behaviour] by managers.

158 The revised cash receipts in March would be $62,200

Month	*March*
Paid in month – 15% × 0.95	5,700
55% in the following month	38,500
30% in 3rd month	18,000
Receipts	62,200

159

Statement 1 is false, it that would be feedback control. Statement 2 is also false, feed-forward control occurs before the activity starts.

	True	False
Feed-forward control systems have an advantage over other types of control in that it establishes how effective planning was.		✓
Feed-forward control occurs while an activity is in progress.		✓

160 The new budgeted production in July would be 9,300 units.

	July
Production budget (units)	
Sales	9,000
Add closing inventory	1,200
Less opening inventory	900
Production	9,300

SHORT TERM COMMERCIAL DECISION MAKING

RELEVANT COSTS AND DECISION MAKING

161 B

The material is in regular use by the organisation and so would be replaced if it is used on the special order. The material is readily available at a price of $3.24 per kg.

Therefore the relevant cost of the material is 1,250 kgs × $3.24 = $4,050.

162 D

Replacement material cost saved (4 kg @ $5.00)	20.00
Less further processing cost ($0.75 × 5 kg)	3.75
Value of M in current use, for each unit made	$16.25

Therefore opportunity cost of using M on the job being tendered for =

$16.25/5 kg = $3.25 per kg.

163 B

The book value is an historic cost and therefore not relevant. There is no intention to replace material X. There are two options for material X, scrap at a value of 50p per kg or use as a replacement for material Y, which would save $4 per kg ($6 – $2). The latter is the preferable option so the relevant cost is $4 per kg for 10 kgs = $40.

164 C

Labour is in short supply so there is an opportunity cost. The contribution from Contract Z will still be earned but will be delayed. The relevant cost is therefore the wages earned plus the penalty fee.

($15 × 100) + ($1,000) = $2,500

165 A

It is cheaper to hire the external consultant for $4,500 rather than pay the $5,000 bonus to the existing junior consultant. The consultant's salary is not a relevant cost as the consultant will still be paid even if the project does not proceed.

166 The expected relevant cost of Material XY for use when evaluating the viability of the contract is $12,900

If contract is carried out and stock is needed, relevant cost is the replacement value of $15,000. Probability = 0.6

If contract is carried out and stock is not needed, relevant cost is the sales value of $12,000. Probability = 0.4

Whatever happens, $900 holding cost is incurred. This will be saved if the contract is carried out.

Expected value = $15,000 × 0.6 + $12,000 × 0.4 – $900 = $12,900.

167 The relevant cost of the 2,000 kgs of material J to be included in the quotation is $16,000

Since material J is in regular use and is readily available in the market, its relevant cost is the replacement price of $8/kg.

So 2,000 kgs × $8/kg = $16,000

168 B

Global businesses may have to adopt different ethical approaches in different markets. What is considered good ethical practice in one country may not be considered ethical in another. This may give a lack of global consistency.

The other statements are true.

169 A

3,700 kg × $3.80 + 500 kg × $6.30 = $17,210

Tutorial note

The company needs 4,200 kg. It has 3,700 kg in stock. It will therefore need to buy 500 kg and these can be bought for $6.30 per kg.

The tricky bit is the value to the company of the 3,700 kg in stock. The $4.50 original purchase price is of course a sunk cost and cannot be relevant.

The stock can be sold for $3.20 per kg, so this is its very minimum value. The stock is worth $3.20 per kg unless the company has an even better alternative.

Well, there is a better alternative. The company can take the stock and, by spending $3.70 per kg on it, can turn it into something worth $7.50 per kg. If something will be worth $7.50 if we spend $3.70 on it, then it is at present worth $3.80. This then is the value of the stock to the company and to fulfil the contract the company will use 3,700 kg of stock with a value of $3.80 per kg.

170 The cost per unit of product Y is $74

By-product revenue = 3,000 × $0.20 = $600.

Therefore costs of the process = $45,000 – $600 = $44,400.

		$
Sales revenue, product X	= 250 × $80 =	20,000
Sales revenue, product Y	= 400 × $100 =	40,000
Total joint product sales revenue =		60,000

Joint costs are apportioned:

To X: $44,400 × 20/60 = $14,800

To Y: $44,400 × 40/60 = $29,600.

Cost per unit of product Y = $29,600/400 = $74.

171 D

$$\$10.50 + \frac{\$10}{2}$$

172 The cost-plus selling price of one unit of product L should be $100

Total annual costs = $60 × 50,000 units = $3,000,000

Required annual return = $10,000,000 × 20% = $2,000,000

Return as a percentage of total cost =2,000,000/3,000,000 = 67%

Required cost-plus selling price = $60 + (67% × $60) = $100

173 A

This would not impact on cash flows. The other options would increase or decrease cash.

174 D

	$/unit
Direct materials	9.00
Direct labour	14.00
Total direct cost	23.00
Production overhead absorbed (2 hours × $4.50 per hour)	9.00
Total production cost	32.00
Mark-up for non-production costs (10% × $32)	3.20
Full cost	35.20
Profit mark-up (20/80 × 35.20)	8.80
Target selling price	44.00

175 The maximum price that a profit-maximising company should be willing to pay to the outside supplier for the components is $40,000

If components are purchased outside:

	$
Contribution earned elsewhere	25,000
Variable cost saving	15,000
Maximum price to pay	40,000

176 D

When making a further processing decision it is necessary to consider incremental revenues and incremental costs. Apportionment of joint costs is NOT relevant to the decision.

177 D

A bad debt provision is an accounting entry and is not a cash flow. It is therefore not relevant for decision making.

The other elements would all be relevant to the decision.

178 A

Full cost can include non-production as well as production costs so the first option is not true. The other options are all disadvantages of using full cost pricing.

179

	Relevant cost?
Accounting adjustments	
Incremental fixed costs	✓

Relevant costs are incremental, future, cash costs. Incremental fixed costs would therefore satisfy this definition. Accounting adjustments such as depreciation is not a cash cost and it would not satisfy this definition.

180 D

Opportunity costs are concerned with identifying the value of any benefit forgone as the result of choosing one course of action in preference to another. They will always be relevant for decision making purposes.

181

	Included?
Prime costs	✓
Direct labour supervision costs	
Variable sales distribution costs	✓
Depreciation on factory machinery	
Selling managers' salaries	

Only variable costs should be included when setting the selling price using marginal cost pricing.

182 The relevant cost of using the material is $460

As the material is not regularly used in the business the inventory should be used. This will be valued at the forgone revenue of $4 per kg, giving a value for the inventory of $160.

The remaining material needs to be purchased at a cost of $15 per kg, $300 in total.

This give a total relevant cost = $160 + $300 = $460.

183 The price per unit to be set in order to achieve the manufacturer's target return on investment is $340

Target return on investment = $500,000 × 12% = $60,000 per annum

Budgeted production and sales = 50 units × 12 months = 600 units

Target return per unit = $60,000/600 units = $100

Full cost = 180 + 40 + 20 = $240

Selling price = $100 + $240 = $340

184

	Correct?
Marginal cost-plus pricing should be only used for short term decision making.	✓
Cost-plus pricing requires that the profit mark-up applied by an organisation is fixed.	
Cost-plus pricing is a strategically focused approach, as it accounts for external factors.	
Full cost-plus pricing requires the budgeted level of output to be determined at the outset.	✓

Statement 1 is correct: Marginal or variable Cost Plus Pricing is not suitable for long term pricing, as recovery of fixed cost may not be possible.

Statements 2 and 3 are not correct: Cost plus pricing is internally focused and a drawback of the technique is that it fails to consider external influence, like competitor pricing strategies.

The mark-up percentage does not have to be fixed: it can vary and be adjusted to reflect market conditions.

Statement 4 is correct: the budgeted level of output does need to be determined for full cost-plus pricing as it would be used to calculate the overhead absorption rate for the calculation of the full cost per unit.

185 The relevant cost of labour is $900

Existing staff are fully employed and cannot be used. The cost of the labour will be the cost of the agency work

= 20 × $45 = $900

186 B

This can be determined by recalculating the budgeted loss for the branch on a relevant cost basis:

	$000
Forgone revenue	(200)
Non-labour variable costs	150
Net labour saving	30
Relevant fixed costs	110
Net benefit of closure	90

The fixed costs should not include the allocated central costs as these will still be incurred even if the branch is closed down. But the rent charge should be included as this will be avoided if the branch is removed.

187 The net benefit from further processing Product Z is $6,000

The joint process costs are not relevant to the decision to further process. The further processing decision will increase revenue by $8,000 ($20 per unit) and will cost $2,000. The overall net benefit will therefore be $6,000.

BREAK EVEN ANALYSIS

188 B

$$\text{Breakeven sales revenue} = \frac{\text{fixed costs}}{\text{C/S ratio}}$$

$$800{,}000 = \frac{\$320{,}000}{\text{C/S ratio}}$$

$$\text{C/S ratio} = \frac{\$320{,}000}{\$800{,}000} = 40\%$$

Sales revenue required to achieve a target profit of $50,000

$$= \frac{\$320{,}000 + 50{,}000}{40\%} = \$925{,}000$$

189 C

Weighted average contribution to sales ratio:

$$\frac{(35\% \times 6) + (20\% \times 5) + (30\% \times 4)}{(6 + 5 + 4)}$$

$$= \frac{(210 + 100 + 120)\%}{15}$$

= 28.667%

Target contribution is obtained by adding back fixed costs to the target profit figure:

$40,000 + $160,000 = $200,000.

Therefore the sales required: 200,000/0.28667 = $697,666 i.e. $698,000 to the nearest $1,000.

190 B

If the margin of safety budgeted in period 3 is 21.015%, then the breakeven number of units in the period is:

6,570 – (6,570 × 21.015%) = 5,189 units

At this level, contribution is equal to the level of fixed costs.

Contribution at this volume is:

5,189 × 35% × $72 = $130,763.

So fixed costs are $130,763 (which is nearest to B, i.e. $131,000).

191

	Required?
The product-specific fixed costs	✓
The product mix ratio	✓
General fixed costs	✓
The method of apportionment of general fixed costs	
Individual product gross contribution to sales ratios	✓

To calculate breakeven, we need total fixed costs (product-specific plus general fixed costs), the C/S ratio for each product and the product sales mix. The method of apportioning fixed costs is irrelevant.

192 A

First calculate the contribution to sales ratio for U:

S	60%	×	⅓	=	20.00%
T	45%	×	⅓	=	15.00%
U	51%	×	⅓	=	17.00% (balancing figure)
Total				=	52.00%

By changing the mix, the overall ratio becomes:

S	60%	×	45%	=	27.00%
T	45%	×	20%	=	9.00%
U	51%	×	35%	=	17.85%
Total				=	53.85%

193 C

The minimum sales values must be satisfied first, earning a contribution of (30% × 400) + (20% × 400) + (25% × 400) = \$300,000. This leaves 850 – 300 = \$550,000 contribution still to be earned before breakeven.

We want to produce the products in the order E, G, F, since this will earn the maximum contribution from the least sales.

Producing the maximum sales of E will generate further contribution of \$(1,200 – 400) × 30% = \$240,000. Thus there is still 550 – 240 = \$310,000 still to be earned.

\$310,000 contribution from G requires sales of $\frac{310}{0.25}$ = \$1,240,000.

The minimum breakeven sales value is therefore:

E (maximum)	1,200
F (minimum)	400
G (minimum + 1,240)	1,640
	3,240

194 The margin of safety is 25.6%

Weighted average C/S ratio equals:

$$\frac{(3 \times 32\%) + (5 \times 48\%)}{3+5} = 42\%$$

$$\text{Breakeven point} = \frac{\text{Fixed costs}}{\text{C/S ratio}} = \frac{\$200{,}000}{0.42} = 476{,}190$$

Margin of safety = \$640,000 – \$476,190 = \$163,810 or 25.6%

195 A

Volume	*Contribution per contract*	*Total contribution*	*Selling price*	*Total revenue*
	$	$	$	$
2	550	1,100	1,000	2,000
3	500	1,500	750	2,250
5	220	1,100	400	2,000
		3,700		6,250

Average C/S ratio $= \dfrac{\$3,700}{\$6,250} = 0.592$

Breakeven point $= \dfrac{\$1,000,000}{0.592} = \$1,689,189$

196 D

Contribution per unit $14 – $6	$8
Breakeven point (BEP) = $24,400 ÷ $8	3,050 units
With new method:	
Contribution per unit $15 – $5	$10
BEP = $31,720 ÷ $10	3,172 units

BEP increases by 122 units

197 The monthly breakeven sales revenue is $594,000

A weighted average contribution to sales (C/S) ratio needs to be calculated:

$$\frac{(3\times 40\%)+(7\times 30\%)+(5\times 35\%)}{3+7+5} = 33.67\%$$

The monthly breakeven sales value is therefore the monthly fixed costs divided by the weighted average C/S ratio:

$200,000/0.3367 = $594,000

198 The minimum contribution that must be earned by a unit of product Y to make it worth producing units of product Y in a profit-maximising budget is $4

Product Y uses more materials per unit than product X. If product X is manufactured, it will earn a contribution of $6 per kilogram consumed and $4 per labour hour. To make product Y worth making, it must earn at least the lower amount of $6 per kilogram ($24 per unit) or $4 per labour hour ($4 per unit). So the answer is $4.

You could possibly work this out by drawing a linear programming graph: if the contribution per unit of Y exceeds $24, the company will make Y only. If the contribution per unit of Y is less than $4, it will make X only. If the contribution per unit of Y is over $4 but less than $24, the optimal production mix will be a combination of X and Y.

199 The percentage increase in the unit variable cost that would result in Product X breaking even at the budgeted level of activity is 30%

Contribution per unit is $10 × 60% = $6. Hence variable cost is $4.

Breakeven point is $120,000 ÷ $6 = 20,000 units.

With a safety margin of 20% the budget was 25,000 units.

Keeping all variables fixed, except the variable cost per unit, we can now find the new variable cost per unit.

Let $x be the variable cost per unit.

If the company is to breakeven at 25,000 units then:

Contribution	=	Fixed costs
($10 – x).25,000 units	=	120,000
x	=	5.20

The new variable cost is $5.20 per unit.

This is $1.20 higher than the original cost, i.e. 30% higher.

200 The break-even sales revenue is $120,000

Variable costs = 70% × $50k = $35k

Contribution = $40k – $35k = $5k

Contribution to sales ratio = $5k/$40k = 12.5%

Fixed costs = 30% × $50k = $15k

Break even sales revenue = $15k/12.5% = $120k

201 The revenue that needs to be generated by Product Z for S plc to achieve the budgeted profit is $16 million

($10m × 0.15) + ($20m × 0.1) + ?m = $5.5m + $2m

$3.5m + ?m = $7.5m   so ? = $4m

Revenue needed to ensure a profit of $2m = 4/0.25 = $16m

202 The target units to break-even is 266 units

Fixed production overhead = $4/unit × 3,000 units = $12,000

Total fixed costs = $12,000 + ($4,000 × 40%) = $13,600

Variable selling costs per unit = ($4,000 × 60%)/3,000 units = $0.80

Total variable costs per unit = $8 + $14 + $6 + $0.80 = $28.80

Contribution per unit = $80 – $28.80 = $51.20

Break even units = $13,600/$51.20 = 266 units

203 C

The P/V line will move down as profit will be lower at all units of sales. The gradient represents the C/S ratio and this will be unchanged.

204 A

The shaded area on the breakeven chart represents loss.

205 The budgeted profit is $160,000

The break even point is = $400,000/$20 = 20,000 units

The margin of safety = 40% × 20,000 units = 8,000 units

Expected profit = 8,000 units × $20 = $160,000

206 The break-even sales revenue is $2,843,000

The weighted average contribution sales ratio can be determined:

Weighted average c/s ratio = $\frac{(\$30 \times 50{,}000) + (\$27 \times 20{,}000)}{(\$40 \times 50{,}000) + (\$45 \text{ x } \times{,}000)}$

= $2,040,000/$2,900,000

= 70.3%

The break even revenue = $2m/70.3% = $2,843,137

207 B

If products are sold in the order of the most favourable contribution to sales ratio, the upper line on the diagram would represent the expected total sales revenue. The point at which it cuts the horizontal axis would represent the break-even point. This is closest to $400,000.

208 B

Assuming products are sold in order of their contribution to sales ratio can help create the profit volume chart, but it is not necessary to assume this when determining the break-even point.

The other statements are valid assumptions of the technique.

209 The break-even sales revenue is $29,000

The weighted average contribution per unit = (70% × 75%) + (30% × 80%) = 76.5%

The break even sales revenue = $22,000/76.5% = $28,758

LINEAR PROGRAMMING

210 The shadow price per litre for material is $1

The original contribution is = (4 × 400) + (2 × 600) = $2,800

The revised contribution is = (4 × 400.5) + (2 × 599.5) = $2,801

The shadow price for materials = 2,801 – 2,800 = $1 per litre

211 B

Break even volume = 7,200 – (7,200 × 26.2%) = 5,314 units

Contribution at break-even point = Fixed costs

Contribution at break-even point = 5,314 × 21% × $56 = $62,493 = Fixed costs

212 B

Linear programming assumes that products are infinitely divisible and that parts of units can be produced and sold.

The other statements are true.

213 D

If, say, X = 400, Y would = 800. The only equation that satisfies these numbers is the correct answer.

214 The highest acceptable price per kg for extra material is $6

This will be the normal price, $4 per kg, plus the shadow price, $2 per kg.

215 C

The optimal production plan will have to be determined by using a simultaneous equations technique.

If the Material X function is multiplied by 2:

Material X: 2A + 4B = 16,000

Material Y: 2A + B = 13,000

Deducting one from the other, leaves:

3B = 3,000

B = 1,000

Substituting this into one of the equations:

2A + (4 × 1,000) = 16,000

2A = 12,000

A = 6,000

216 A

Each unit of A (X) requires 5 hours of skilled labour so the equation must contain 5X. Each unit of B (Y) requires 1 hour of skilled labour so the equation must contain 1Y.

217 C

A shadow price for a scarce resource is its opportunity cost. It is the amount of contribution that would be lost if one unit less of that resource were available. It is similarly the amount of additional contribution that would be earned if one unit more of that resource were available. (This is on the assumption that the scarce resource is available at its normal variable cost.)

218 A

Product cost per unit		*E1*		*E2*		*E3*		*E4*
		$		$		$		$
Conversion costs		40		65		65		55
Less general fixed costs absorbed	0.5 × $30	15	0.5 × $30	15	0.6 × $30	18	0.6 × $30	18
Variable conversion cost		25		50		47		37
Material cost		24		33		41		30
Total variable cost		49		83		88		67
Selling price		90		112		123		103
Contribution		41		29		35		36
Contribution for each $1		1.7		0.8		0.8		1.2
spent on material		1		8		5		0
Ranking		1st		3rd		4th		2nd

219 D

The company maximises contribution by producing Qutwo. Contribution per unit of material is:

$\frac{\$8.50}{2.5\text{kg}}$ = $3.40 and this is the shadow price.

220 D

	R	*S*	*T*
	$	$	$
Contribution per unit			
$(100 – 15 – 20 – 15)	50		
$(150 – 30 – 35 –20)		65	
$(160 – 25 – 30 – 22)			83
Direct labour cost per unit	20	35	30
Contribution per $1 of direct labour	2.50	1.85	2.77
Profitability ranking	2nd	3rd	1st

221 C

If S1 is unlimited then the products must be ranked on the basis of their contribution per machine hour:

			Ranking
X1	\$12/6 = \$2.00		2nd
X2	\$5/4 = \$1.25		3rd
X3	\$8/3 = \$2.66		1st
			Hours required
Minimum X2	100 × 4	400	
Produce X3	200 × 3	600 = a total of 1,000 hours used 7,000 hours remaining	
Produce X1	$\frac{7,000}{6}$	= 1,166	

222 The minimum total cost at which BJS Company can obtain the full requirement of components is \$563,000

Calculate extra cost per hour if buy externally.

	P \$	*Q* \$	*R* \$
Internal cost	45	70	56
External cost	65	78	80
Extra cost	20	8	24
Hours per unit	9	5	12
Extra cost per hour	\$2.22	\$1.60	\$2.00

To minimise cost make P internally, then R and finally Q.

	Units	*Total hours*	*Cost per unit*	*Total cost*
P – internal	3,000	27,000	\$45	\$135,000
R – internal	1,916	23,000	\$56	\$107,296
R – external	1,084		\$80	\$86,720
Q – external	3,000		\$78	\$234,000
Total		**50,000**		**\$563,016**

223

	Shadow price >0?
Direct labour hours	✓
Material A	
Material B	
Machine hours	

Only resources that meet at the optimal point will have a shadow price. This is at point B, where the direct labour line meets line R. The other constraints lines are above this point and there therefore must be slack in these resources which could be put to other uses. Resources that have a slack do not have a shadow price.

224

	Meal?
Most profitable	L
Least profitable	K

	K	*L*	*M*
Sales price	\$5.00	\$3.00	\$4.40
Less variable costs	\$3.60	\$1.80	\$3.15
Contribution per meal	\$1.40	\$1.20	\$1.25
Minutes	÷ 10	÷ 4	÷ 8
Contribution per minute	\$0.14	\$0.30	\$0.16

225

	Limitation?
Linear relationships must exist	✓
There can only be two products	✓
There can only be two scarce resources	
All variables must be completely divisible	✓
A computer must be used to find the optimal point	

Linear programming can cope with any number of constraints and the solution does not always need to be solved by a computer.

226 B

This should be based on contribution per unit:

Product	*J*	*L*
	$/unit	$/unit
Selling price	115	120
Direct material A ($10 per kg)	20	10
Direct material B ($6 per kg)	12	24
Skilled labour ($14 per hour)	28	21
Variable overhead ($4 per machine hour)	14	18
Contribution	41	47

And the iso-contribution line is 41J + 47L = M

227 The maximum amount of Material A available is 2,000 kgs

The line crosses the horizontal axis at coordinates T = 0 and R = 1,000. If each unit of R takes 2 kgs of Material A, then there must be 2,000 kgs of Material A available.

228 C

The optimal production plan will have to be determined by using a simultaneous equations technique.

If the Material X function is multiplied by 2:

Material X: 2A + 4B = 16,000

Material Y: 2A + B = 13,000

Deducting one from the other, leaves:

3B = 3,000

B = 1,000

Substituting this into one of the equations:

2A + (4 × 1,000) = 16,000

2A = 12,000

A = 6,000

229 The maximum number of units of Product B which can be produced is 60 units.

If all of the resources have less than or equal to constraints then the feasible region cannot exceed the lowest of the lines on the diagram. This means that the maximum number of units of Product B that can be produced can be no higher than where this line meets the vertical axis which is at 60 units.

230 The number of units of Product Y produced in order to maximise contribution (to the nearest whole unit) is 8,000 units.

The optimal production plan will have to be determined by using a simultaneous equations technique.

If the unskilled labour function is multiplied by 3:

Skilled labour: $6X + 4Y \leq 62,000$

Unskilled labour: $6X + 15Y \leq 150,000$

Deducting one from the other, leaves:

$11Y = 88,000$

$Y = 8,000$

DEALING WITH UNCERTAINTY IN THE SHORT TERM

231 If orders must be placed before the daily demand is known, the number of units that should be purchased at the beginning of each day in order to maximise expected profit is 200 units

Produce a payoff table:

Demand	*Probability*		*Supply*	
		100	*200*	*300*
100 units	0.25	\$400	\$0 (W1)	(\$400) (W2)
200 units	0.40	\$400	\$800	\$400 (W3)
300 units	0.35	\$400	\$800	\$1,200

Workings

(W1)	100 × \$8 – 200 × \$4	=	\$0
(W2)	100 × \$8 – 300 × \$4	=	(\$400)
(W3)	200 × \$8 – 300 × \$4	=	\$400

Expected profits:

If supply 100 units, EVs	=	\$400
If supply 200 units, EV = \$0 × 0.25 + \$800 × 0.4 + \$800 × 0.35	=	\$600
If supply 300 units, EV = (\$400) × 0.25 + \$400 × 0.4 + \$1,200 × 0.35	=	\$480

Therefore, profit is maximised by supplying 200 units.

232 The probability that the weekly contribution will exceed $20,000 is 45%

To generate a contribution greater than $20,000 it is necessary to earn a unit contribution greater than $20. Consider each of the feasible combinations:

Selling price	*Variable cost*	*Contribution*	*Probability*
$	$	$	
50	20	30	0.45 × 0.55 = 0.2475
60	20	40	0.25 × 0.55 = 0.1375
60	30	30	0.25 × 0.25 = 0.0625
		Answer =	**0.4475**

Answer = 44.75% = 45% to nearest full %

233 B

Project	*EV*	**Workings**
	$000	
L	500	(500 × 0.2) + (470 × 0.5) + (550 × 0.3)
M	526	(400 × 0.2) + (550 × 0.5) + (570 × 0.3)
N	432.5	(450 × 0.2) + (400 × 0.5) + (475 × 0.3)
O	398	etc.
P	497.5	

Therefore, Project M will maximise expected cash.

234 Assuming the baker adopts the minimax regret decision rule, the number of batches of bread that he should bake each day is 12 batches

Contribution table		*Daily demand*		
		10	*11*	*12*
	10 (W1)	500	500	500
Batches baked	11 (W2)	480	550	550
	12 (W3)	460	530	600

Workings

(W1) If 10 batches are baked they will all be sold earning a contribution of $500

(W2) If 11 batches are baked and 10 are sold this earns a contribution of 10 × 50 – 20 = 480

(W3) If 12 batches are baked and 10 are sold contribution = 10 × 50 – 40 = 460

A regret table can now be produced which shows the shortfall from the maximum contribution that could be earned at each demand level. So, if demand is 12 batches, the maximum contribution is $600. If only 10 batches are baked, the contribution earned is $500, a regret of $100.

Regret table		*Daily demand*			
		10	*11*	*12*	*Max. Regret*
	10	0	50	100	100
Batches baked	11	20	0	50	50
	12	40	20	0	40

So to minimise the maximum regret the baker should bake 12 batches.

235

Decision criteria	*Attitude to risk*
Expected values	Risk neutral
Maximax	Risk seeker
Maximin	Risk averse
Minimax regret	Risk averse

236 A

The expected value is

= −2m + [(0.8 × 9.2m) + (0.2 × −1m)] = $5.16m

237 The probability that the variance is less than $45,000 is 0.13%

The mean is $60,000. $45,000 is $15,000 away from the mean.

This represents $15,000/$5,000 = 3.00 standard deviations. This is the z score.

From tables, on the left hand column, look up the z score to one decimal place, i.e. 3.0. Look along this row until it meets the column with the 2nd decimal place (0.00). The table gives us 0.4987.

This means that when looking at the 50% of variances that are below the mean 49.87% of them are within 3 standard deviations. Therefore, the probability that the variance will be below $45,000 is the remaining 0.13%

238 B

Minimax regret table:

	Order level			
Demand	20 bunches	30 bunches	40 bunches	50 bunches
20 bunches	$0	$40 **	$80	$120
30 bunches	$30	$0	$40	$80
40 bunches	$60	$30	$0	$40
50 bunches	$90	$60	$30	$0

*** Working:*

If demand is 20 bunches, the optimum order level would have been 20 bunches. In this situation a profit of $60 would have been made (as per payoff table). This is the maximum profit available for a demand of 20.

If Chris had ordered 30 bunches instead of 20 then he would have ordered too many and would have made a profit of just $20, therefore the value of the regret is the difference between the optimum profit and the actual profit. In this case the regret would be $60 – $20 = $40.

The maximum regret for 20 bunches is $90

The maximum regret for 30 bunches is $60

The maximum regret for 40 bunches is $80

The maximum regret for 50 bunches is $120

If the company wishes to minimise the maximum regret 30 bunches should be ordered.

239 A

The value of perfect information =

Expected profit with the information – expected profit without the information.

In this scenario the value of the perfect information is $15,000.

The expected profit without the information is $142,000.

Therefor the expected profit with the information is $142,000 + $15,000 = $157,000

240 A

Perfect information is always 100% accurate. By comparison imperfect information is usually correct but can be incorrect.

241 The probability that lowering the selling price to $45 per unit would increase profit is 82%

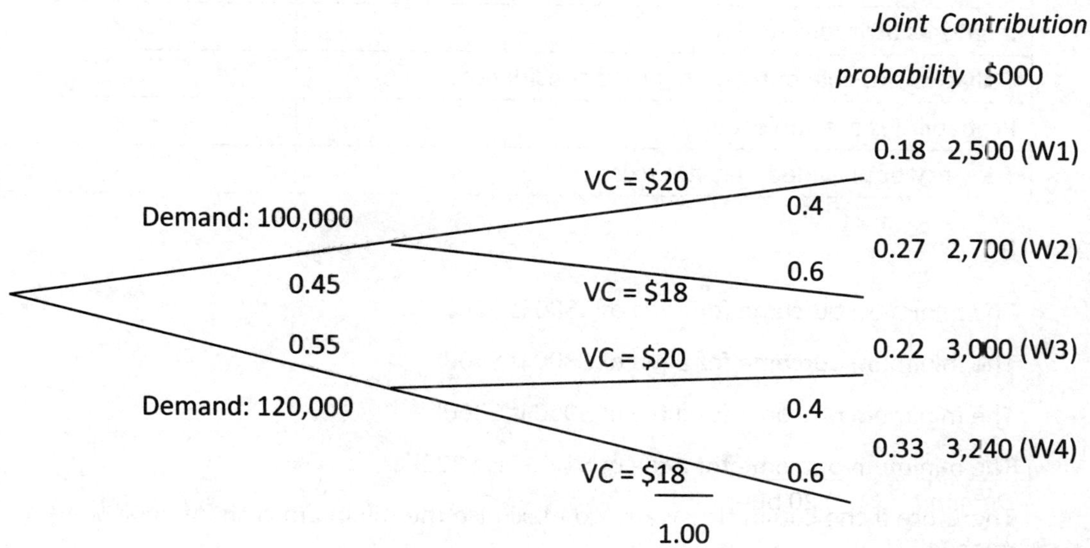

Existing contribution = ($50 – $21) × 90,000 units = 2,610 ($000)

Contribution is greater than this in (W2), (W3) and (W4) above.

∴ The probability of the profit being higher is = 0.27 + 0.22 + 0.33 = 0.82

Workings

(W1) ($45 – $20) × 100,000 units

(W2) ($45 – $18) × 100,000 units

(W3) ($45 – $20) × 120,000 units

(W4) ($45 – $18) × 120,000 units

242 D

Expected selling price			*Expected cost*
	$		$
$20 × 0.25	5	$8 × 0.2	1.6
$25 × 0.4	10	$10 × 0.5	5
330 × 0.35	10.5	$12 × 0.3	3.6
	25.5		10.2

Expected unit contribution = $25.50 – $10.20 = $15.30 × 1,000 = $15,300

243 Which of the following are disadvantages of using an expected value technique?

	Disadvantage of EVs?
Expected values only provides the most likely result	
It ignores attitudes to risk	✓
Only two possible outcomes can be considered	
Probabilities are subjective	✓
The answer provided may not exist	✓

244 B

The minimum outcome for a fee of $600 is $360k

The minimum outcome for a fee of $800 is $400k

The minimum outcome for a fee of $900 is $360k

The minimum outcome for a fee of $1,000 is $320k

Therefore if the committee wants to maximise the minimum cash inflow it will set a fee of $800.

245 The number of cakes Sarah should bake if she applies the maximax decision criterion is 30.

If Sarah applied the maximax decision criterion she would bake 30 cakes each day as the maximum contribution of $21 is to be gained at this level.

246 D

If market condition is forecast as Poor, then Project P should be chosen as this project yields the highest cash flow under a poor market.

However, if the market condition is forecast as Good or Excellent, then Project M should be chosen as M will yield the highest cash.

In summary:

Market condition	*Selected project*	*Cash (x) $000*	*Probability (p)*	*px*
Poor	P	600	0.20	120
Good	M	550	0.50	275
Excellent	M	570	0.30	171
			1.00	566

Expected return with perfect information	$566,000
Expected return without (answer to 1.2)	$526,000
∴ Value of information	$40,000

247 B

The maximum regret for product W is $43,000

The maximum regret for product X is $17,000

The maximum regret for product Y is $73,000

The maximum regret for product Z is $38,000

248 B

Point G represents a decision point. If the decision is taken to licence then there is a value of $6m.

The other decision is to further invest – which appears to have a cost of $4m. But this then opens up the chance point where there is a 70% chance of making $22m and a 30% chance of making $9m. So this decision to further invest would have an expected value of:

$= -4m + [(0.7 \times 22) + (0.3 \times 9)] = \$14.1m$

Therefore, the decision to further invest is worth more than the licencing option. The company would choose to invest and would make $14.1m.

249 The maximum amount that should be paid for the information from the market research company is $7,500.

The value of perfect information is calculated as:

Expected value with perfect information – Expected value without perfect information.

Expected value without perfect information:

The expected value without perfect information is $880,000.

Expected value with perfect information:

Demand	**Sales price**	**Profit (x)**	**Prob (p)**	**px**
High	$105	$1,725,000	30%	$517,500
Medium	$100	$700,000	50%	$350,000
Low	$100	$100,000	20%	$20,000
			EV	**$887,500**

The value of perfect information is $887,500 – $880,000 = $7,500

250 C

The information provided by the meteorologist is called imperfect information. The value of imperfect information is calculated in the same way as the value of perfect information:

Expected profit with the information – expected profit without the information.

In this scenario we already know the value of the information: Soggy is prepared to pay $30,000 for the information.

We have also been told that the expected profit with the information is $1,250,000.

We therefore have to calculate the expected profit without the information:

= $1,250,000 – $30,000 = $1,220,000

251 The maximum amount that should be paid for the information from the market research company is $11,440.

The value of perfect information is calculated as:

Expected value with perfect information – Expected value without perfect information.

Expected value without perfect information:

The expected value without perfect information is $719,700.

Expected value with perfect information:

Demand	*Shop size*	*Profit (x)*	*Prob (p)*	*px*
Strong	LARGE	1,413,200	0.2	282,640
Good	LARGE	865,700	0.4	346,280
Weak	MEDIUM	255,550	0.4	102,220
			Expected value	731,140

The value of perfect information is $731,140 – $719,700 = $11,440

252 The number of cakes Sarah should bake if she applies the maximin decision criterion is 20.

	Number of cakes baked		
	20	25	30
Worst contribution	$14	$11.5	$9

If Sarah baked 20 cakes the worst contribution would be $14, this is the best "worst contribution"

If Sarah applied the maximax decision criterion she would bake 30 cakes each day as the maximum contribution of $21 is to be gained at this level.

253 A

A regret matrix is shown below:

	Membership level		
Membership fee	*Low* $000	*Average* $000	*High* $000
$600	40	0	0
$800	0	40	60
$900	40	75	45
$1,000	80	100	120

Maximum regret if set fee of $600 is $40k

Maximum regret if set fee of $800 is $60k

Maximum regret if set fee of $900 is $75k

Maximum regret if set fee of $1,000 is $120k

To minimise the maximum regret a fee of $600 should be set.

254 The expected value of the company profit if the selling price is reduced to $45 per unit is $1,708,200

Expected demand:	
(100,000 × 0.45) + (120,000 × 0.55)	111,000 units
Expected variable cost:	
($20 × 0.40) + ($18 × 0.60)	$18.80
Contribution per unit:	
$45 – $18.80	$26.20
Expected contribution:	
111,000 × $26.20	$2,908,200
Less fixed costs	($1,200,000)
Expected profit	$1,708,200

255 The expected value at point A on the decision trees (to the nearest $0.1m) is $22m

Point A represents a decision point. If the decision is taken to outsource then there is a value of $22m.

The other decision is to further invest – which appears to have a cost of $20m. But this then opens up the chance point where there is a 60% chance of making $60m and a 40% chance of making $12m. So this decision to further invest would have an expected value of:

= –20m + [(0.6 × 60) + (0.4 × 12)] = $20.8m

Therefore, the decision to further invest is worth less than the outsourcing option. The company would choose to outsource and would make $22m.

256 C

Monthly contribution will exceed $13,500 if unit contribution exceeds $13.50. This will be the case for the following combinations:

Sales price	*Variable cost*	*Probability*	*Joint probability*
$25	$8	0.4 × 0.2	0.08
$25	$10	0.4 × 0.5	0.20
$30	($8)		
$30	($10)	0.35 × 1	0.35
$30	($12)		
Total			0.63

257 Using expected values, the financial benefit from engaging MS for the concert is $915

The expected audience size = (0.5 × 300) + (0.3 × 400) + (0.2 × 500) = 370

The expected contribution = 370 × [(0.7 × 25) + (0.3 × 40)] = $10,915

The financial benefit from engaging MS is $10,915 – $10,000 = $915

Therefore it is worthwhile engaging MS for the concert.